For John & Teri Hall

With best wishes for
your continued success
in your "web lifestyle"
and your web-lifestyle-based
business.

Frank Feather

future living

The Coming Web Lifestyle

future living

The Coming Web Lifestyle

Frank Feather

Best-Selling Author of Future Consumer.Com

Warwick Publishing
www.warwickgp.com

Future Living: The Coming "Web Lifestyle"
© 2003, Frank Feather and Glocal Marketing Consultants,
P.O. Box 38, Aurora, Ontario, Canada, L4G-3H1
Tel: (905) 642-9090; Fax: (905) 642-9091
www.future-trends.com

We acknowledge the financial support of the Government of Canada through the Book Publishing Industry Development Program for our publishing activities.

ISBN: 1-894622-28-6

Published in North America by Warwick Publishing Inc.
161 Frederick Street, Toronto, Ontario M5A 4P3 Canada
www.warwickgp.com

Distributed in Canada by
Canadian Book Network
c/o Georgetown Terminal Warehouses
34 Armstrong Avenue, Georgetown, Ontario L7G 4R9
www.canadianbooknetwork.com

Distributed in the United States by
Weatherhill
41 Monroe Turnpike, Trumbull, Connecticut 06611 U.S.A.

Cover design and layout: Kimberley Young
Author Photo: Bernard Prost, B. Prost Photography Inc., Toronto
www.portfolios.com/photog/prost.b
Printed and bound in Canada

For Our Children

May they and their children,
and their children's children,
enjoy a successful "Web Lifestyle"
in a peaceful and prosperous world.

CONTENTS

Introduction

FUTURE LIVING
The Coming Web Lifestyle

If we could first know where we are, and whither we are tending, we could better judge what to do and how to do it.

Abraham Lincoln

L ifestyles change with history. And history will record September 11, 2001, as a major turning point that convinced most people in North America to adopt a new lifestyle — a Web Lifestyle.

When such a major event fits long-term trends already underway, it is easier to see the future. Certainly, 9/11 stopped us in our tracks, leaving us disoriented and looking for direction. And in that you're reading this book, you already sense that sweeping change is in the air — and are wondering where we are and what to do about it.

The kaleidoscope of life was thoroughly shaken on 9/11. And the pieces are still in flux. But when they settle they will reveal a brand new future for all of us. And we need to find ways to connect with that new future.

So we need to figure out where the global forces (or "G-Forces") of change and the tides of time are tending to take us — and how to respond.

THE TIDES OF TIME

Abraham Lincoln's three-part rhetorical question quoted above is most relevant to today's dilemma. Here again are his three questions, along with answers to be further explained.

> **1. Where are we?** We are at a major turning point in history.
>
> **2. Whither are we tending?** We are moving rapidly through turbulent times to a stable, networked society that will be remarkably different than the prevailing way of life.
>
> **3. What might we do about it?** Now, more than ever, it is time to rally around our families and adopt a brand new lifestyle — a "Web Lifestyle."

1. Where Are We?

So where are we? The evidence of big change is everywhere. Our world already was changing dramatically during the months surrounding the turn of the millennium. America alone experienced many major events of compound significance: seemingly random school and public shootings, corporate failures and ethical lapses of a size previously unimagined, corruption and patronage eroding trust in elected officials, soaring gas prices, soaring unemployment, soaring deficits, 9/11, and war.

These and other social, technical, economic, and political G-Forces of change (discussed and explained below) are all part of a mega-shift to a new way of life.

Many people thought the 2000 turn of the millennium would mark revolutionary change. But it wasn't a true turning point; just another day on the calendar. Other than going to a 2000 New Year's party, most people saw it as nothing more than the start of another year. And prior to 9/11 most people had no clue what was going on outside their own insular lives — and didn't much care so long as their car's gas tank was filled.

History rarely shows its complete hand except in retrospect. But there can be no doubt that 9/11 was a genuine turning point. True turning points cause a mass shift in public consciousness. After 9/11 a jittery quiet took over America and civilized societies everywhere. And 9/11 will forever be etched on our minds and recorded as the day when most people's lives changed and we entered a different future. It was a seismic event. And its aftershocks will ripple around the world for decades.

For sure, every child born on that day and since was born into a new world. Indeed, they mark the start of a new generation that will grow up and live with values very different than those of all previous generations.

That's where we are.

2. Whither Are We Tending?

The G-Forces of change, of which terrorism is but one, have brought us into the Internet age. G-Forces interact on each other to create a four-stage "MegaCycle," shown on the next page.

Let's first understand the G-Force MegaCycle in *general* principle. Then in Part I of the book we'll explore the *specific* G-Forces at play today.

Stage 1 — Social Motivation

The first stage in the MegaCycle is initiated by us. Fundamental to

FOUR-STAGE MEGACYCLE

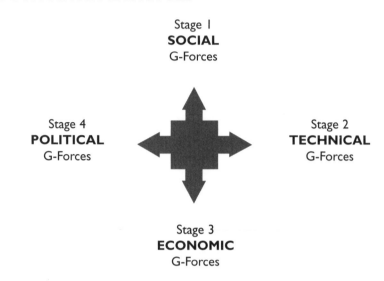

Stage 1
SOCIAL
G-Forces

Stage 4
POLITICAL
G-Forces

Stage 2
TECHNICAL
G-Forces

Stage 3
ECONOMIC
G-Forces

Source: G-Forces by Frank Feather; New York: William Morrow, 1989.

all G-Forces is the overriding behavior of ordinary people: our needs, our aspirations, and our ideas. Little improves in the world unless you and I decide to change things. As we move up through Abraham Maslow's hierarchy of needs — oxygen-water-food, clothing-shelter-safety, socialization, self-esteem, self-actualization — we generate new ideas to sustain progress. As each new generation brings fresh ideas and values to bear, society literally regenerates itself. As new ideas catch on, they travel like lightning — especially now with the Internet — changing the aspirations of a wider population. And so the cycle of social change repeats, rippling across the world as new generations of people come to power.

Stage 2 — Technical Innovation

Fresh ideas spur research and development that constantly push back the frontiers of scientific knowledge to spawn further advances. Technology thus also regenerates itself and we tend to talk of new generations of technology, with new versions making earlier ones obsolete. The car thus replaced the horse as a mode of transport. The clearest examples today are microchips, software, and the Web. The more efficient and productive a new technology, the greater are the economic and social benefits for us all to enjoy. All the wealth ever created has come from better efficiency and productivity. So we need to adopt the latest and most powerful technologies, both to boost the economy and to enhance national and personal security. And today, that means embracing the Web.

Stage 3 — Economic Modernization

The third stage, then, is the effective use of technology to restructure and modernize our socio-economic infrastructure. This is achieved by marshalling the planet's resources and managing the environment while orchestrating the production and distribution of wealth on a long-term sustainable basis. Sadly, we often are reluctant to let go of entrenched ways and are too slow to see the benefits of the new. Economists rarely point the way. Intoxicated with data about the past, many of them ignore predictable cycles and seem unable to forecast with any accuracy. They fall back on short-term data much like a drunkard grasps a lamp post — to support outmoded ideas, not to illuminate the future. In reality, as we shall see, a 57-year long-wave MegaCycle is in play and the economy is set to boom again for at least the next 20 years.

Stage 4 — Political Reformation

Finally, to ensure we benefit from technical innovation and economic progress, the political process must rise to a higher level of human aspiration. If not, history shows that people will be unhappy and will rebel. Hence, political processes and governments inevitably get reformed — preferably by consensus but by social upheaval and revolution if need be. Unfortunately, politicians usually are the last to see and do anything. Grasping to power, they struggle to maintain the status quo. They "spin" themselves so dizzy struggling to explain the past and the present that they are unable to offer even a blurred vision of the future. Faced with global terrorism, freedom and democracy are under attack. And how we practice democracy is out of sync with our new world. To win the battle for freedom, and bring people back to the political process, we need to move quickly to a system of electronic democracy from home via the Internet.

Seeing the "Big Picture"

To anticipate how these groups of G-Forces are transfiguring the kaleidoscope of life, you need to see the big picture. To figure out what on Earth is going on, you need to mentally sit on the Moon.

Let your mind circle Earth via the Moon and you gain a completely fresh insight into the human condition and your own place in the overall scheme of things. This phenomenon has struck every astronaut sent aloft. If you mentally go into orbit, you will see all the chaos and all the order, all the idiocy and all the genius, all the problems and all the opportunities.

Since no situation is static, we also need to see the world in motion over the long term. We therefore also need to think futuristically; to perceive the long-term G-Forces and anticipate their shifts and potential interactions. These rhythms have a universal source, the force of which reflects itself in human behavior — and thus in very evident long-wave G-Forces worldwide.

G-Forces are almost inevitable, near certainties. That's not to say the future is predetermined. To a large degree, the future is subject to our will — if we anticipate the G-Forces. Then we might avoid or try to deflect them, manage them, or try to change their direction and effect. Remember, all G-Forces start with human actions.

Nor do trends go in straight lines: The future always contains ups and downs, zigzags, and a few so-called wild-card or unanticipated events. For example, 9/11 was not anticipated, even by U.S. intelligence. But it should have been foreseen as one possible scenario of global terrorism, which has been a growing G-Force for more than 20 years. It thus was not a true wild-card event but — as we have since learned — a massive intelligence, security, and foreign policy failure.

That said, the tragedy brought us to a new future, detailed in the Preview chapter that follows this one. But generally speaking, what kind of future will it be?

Mega-Reversal to Pre-Industrial Values

The MegaCycle often makes some old ways obsolete while reviving others. The Internet Age is in fact reversing many life elements, and the future will reflect many aspects of life in the pre-Industrial era. This "reversal" effect is a recurrent theme of this book.

Marshall McLuhan, in his 1963 masterpiece, *Understanding Media*, said any new medium has four inter-related effects. It will

- **Enhance**   (amplify, inflate, play up) some aspects of life;

- **Obsolesce**   (impede, erode, replace, push aside,
                    or play down) some aspects of life;
- **Revive**   (retrieve, replay, or bring back) what was
                    previously obsolesced; and
- **Transform**   (reverse or flip) when pushed to extremes.

Thus, for example, cars enhanced privacy and obsolesced the horse and buggy. They also revived the countryside as people took weekend drives there, only to then transform it into sprawling bedroom communities as the city revived as a workplace.

McLuhan predicted that "global electric media" — such as today's Internet which, of course, didn't exist at the time he wrote — would speed up everything to real-time simultaneity, erode time and distance, revive human communication on a planet-wide basis, and put everybody and everything immediately in touch.

In sum, the Internet Revolution (or "Webolution") will reverse all previous processes and flip the old order of life and society on its head (see table opposite).

The Webolution makes the industrial-era corporate factory model of "mass" obsolete. Instead, it brings out the entrepreneurial and innovative, value-adding, intellectual capital that "prosumer" individuals and families bring to the economic process. They will produce and consume most of their own products and services, placing them — not corporations — at the center of wealth creation.

"Back-to-the-Future" Families

The Webolution's reversal effect returns us to a family structure more like that of the Agricultural Age when life was home-based.

Families were large and depended on kinship ties. People tended

THE THREE MAIN SOCIO-ECONOMIC ERAS

Self-Consuming Agricultural Era (Farms)	Mass-Producing Industrial Era (Factories)	"Prosuming" Internet Era (Digital Homes)
Custom-tailored items made one-by-one, by hand, by farm families and craftsmen, in rural areas.	Mass-produced items made by machine, in batches, in company-owned factories and office complexes, in urban centers.	Mass-customized item made one-by-one, on the Web, in real-time, by e-businesses or by home-based webpreneurs and "prosumer" families.
Self-consumed or sold in local village market or local artisans' own shops, often operated out of the home.	Sold to consumers in main street stores and suburban malls in local, national and global mass markets.	Self-consumed by prosumers, or sold by them to other prosumers in "glocal" network markets online.
Sales generated via local "word-of-mouth" recommendation, with no need to advertise.	Sales generated using mass-media advertising, mass marketing, and promotions.	Sales generated via "word-of-modem" and one-to-one relationships, not advertising.
Agri-husbandry, manual labor, and craftsmanship skills.	Machine-tending labor and engineering skills.	Knowledge synthesis, creativity, innovation, and brain-power skills.
Own or lease land; own your own labor, skill and time. Plough back the profits.	Own capital and assets, buying labor as needed. Pay dividend and re-invest.	Own your own labor, intellectual capital and time. Retain all profits, investing the surplus.

to live in large, close-knit, multi-generational families, with grandparents living under the same roof. Uncles, aunts, in-laws, and cousins lived in next-door cottages or on neighboring farms. Each family grouping worked together as a self-sufficient economic production and consumption unit.

Families were immobile — rooted in the soil — and life's daily tasks were done in and around the home. Children were educated at home and the sick and elderly were treated and cared for at home. There were no external childcare or eldercare providers except extended family members and neighbors who came to help.

Relatives and neighbors helped each other to scythe fields of hay, rake it into windrows, shake it out to dry, and harvest it into the barn — all by hand. But this was not "work" — there was no such concept. The farmer didn't say he was "going to work" but to "rake the hay," or "milk the cows," or "collect the eggs."

Farms and cottages also began turning out "manufactures" (manmade crafts, textiles, and other products) long before there were any factory-based manufacturers. Nobody went to a separate workplace. But there were constant close encounters with neighbors, either out in the fields or at the village market.

Back then, not even the village idiot would have forecast that the fields would one day be harvested with a combine, let alone be built over with factories and homes. But the Industrial Revolution swiftly shifted work to factories, and later to factory-like office buildings. Kids went to factory-like schools, the sick were put in factory-like hospitals, and the elderly confined to nursing homes.

Likewise today: few can imagine most of us spending our time at home rather than commuting to offices, going to schools, or shopping in supermarkets. Yet a whole set of G-Forces are converging to transfer life's locus back into the home.

Bye-Bye, "Bread Winner"

The industrial-era workplace separated bread-winner husband and homemaker child-rearing wife. That set-up will soon be a vestige of history. The work–family divide is being replaced by a new work–family pact where the Webolution makes the home again central to society.

The "Web Lifestyle" family will do most things together at home, sharing both household chores and tasks of economic production that generate family income. Many households may again employ live-in or visiting servants and caregivers of various kinds. Future households will be electronically extended families that network with other families — next door and across the world.

Paradoxically, this shift back to the home actually started when women moved out into the workplace in the 1960s and 1970s. By the 1980s, the resulting "dual-income-with-kids-you-never-see" created a desire to have work and family as mutually reinforcing parts of a balanced life. Yet, a mid-1999 opinion poll showed that only 30 percent of North Americans thought they had achieved a satisfactory work–life balance. Indeed, 63 percent said they would work fewer hours if they could find a way to do so.

As a result, there is a growing urge among people to work at home, often for themselves. For sure, the loyalty tie that bound people to employers is broken. People simply expect and demand both greater autonomy and more concern for their individual interests. While the old media still present workplace and career images for which some

9 EPIC CHANGES IN FAMILY LIFESTYLE ACTIVITIES

Activity	Agricultural Era	Industrial Era	Internet Era
1. Work	Family Farm, Home Workshop	Factory, Office Building	Home Office, Mobile
2. Shop	Make Yourself, Village Market	Town Stores, Shopping Mall	Internet Stores, Shopping Mall,
3. Money	Barter, Cash	Banks, Brokers	Digital Cash, e-Wallets
4. School	At-Home Tutor, School House	K-12 Schools, Universities	Home Schooling, Online Courses
5. Health	Herb Garden, House Calls	Doctor's Office, Hospital	Tele-Medicine, e-House Calls
6. Fun	Make Your Own	Radio/TV, Film	e-Fun @ Home
7. Religion	Bible, Church	Church, TV	e-Congregation
8. Politics	Feudal Lord	Parliament	e-Voting
9. Business	Family Farm, Craftsmen	Corporate Employee	Family-Run e-Business

people still strive, the Web lets families pursue their own interests together and with like-minded people worldwide. Life becomes home-based but cyber-spaced.

Reversal of Family Activities

In many ways, then, the Webolution revives or returns us to a modern-day version of the home-based, family-owned, customized production and consumption model of pre-industrial times, transforming the structure of family and community life.

The table opposite shows how the Industrial Revolution changed various family activities and how the Webolution reverses them. Part II of this book examines these activities as the "Nine Ways of the Web Lifestyle" that point to a brand new future for us all.

3. What Might We Do About It?

In the final analysis, it's not so much what *will* happen but what we *do* about it. If we take the proper steps, then a better family life, increased personal and national security, and constantly improving prosperity are all attainable.

However, though life will revert to pre-industrial aspects, we won't return to the pre-9/11 "normal." Rather, as will be explained, we will go forward to a "better normal" way of life.

On top of the specific G-Forces detailed in the next chapter, the 9/11 nightmare cast uncertainty into our lives and caused deep anxiety over the future. That makes it harder to keep a strong faith in our future. But let us never forget that we are an optimistic, confident, and successful society.

We *will* achieve our dreams!

Now is no time for pessimism and trepidation. Now is the time for courage and clear-headed thinking; to understand what's really changing and how to respond.

For starters, most people spend way too much time "making a living" rather than "living a life."

Many don't even know who lives next door. They say they don't have enough time. Not so! Day in, day out, we collectively waste millions of hours of precious time. Think about it:

- Commuting to work in stop-and-go traffic
- Driving around searching for a parking spot
- Stuck at red lights or in gridlock
- Waiting for trains, buses, and airplanes
- Waiting for elevators and riding them up and down
- Driving kids to and from school
- Waiting in line at retail checkouts
- Waiting in line at post offices
- Waiting in bank teller and banking machine line-ups
- Sitting in hospital and doctors' waiting rooms
- Waiting … waiting … waiting …

The list goes on. Life has become a wasteful series of waiting in lines or going places. This unnecessary daily tedium of coming and going leaves us no time for ourselves or our families.

Run ragged, we have no life. Having no life is what happens to you if you waste time. That's dumb!

Thanks to the Internet, of course, we actually don't need to "go" anywhere to complete most daily tasks. For example:

- You don't go to work, work comes to you.
- You don't go to the library, the library comes to you.

- You don't go to the bank, the bank comes to you.
- You don't go to the store, the store comes to you.
- You don't go to school, the school comes to you.
- You don't go to the doctor, the doctor comes to you.
- You don't go to the voting booth, the booth comes to you.

Everything gets reversed: they all come to you over the Web.

Rather than going out and wasting valuable time waiting "in line," futuristic families simply stay home and go "online." They adopt some or all of the "Nine Ways of the Web Lifestyle."

Those who live their lives through the Web find they have abundant quality time for their families and a much better life. They take some or all of these simple steps to win back their time and future-proof their lives by embracing a Web Lifestyle.

They get a Web Life!

THE WEB LIFESTYLE
Home-Based, Cyber-Spaced

Families and lifestyles always change over time. Today, the out-moded factory-based model of family life and society is severely strained if not broken.

We're living through the collapse of an outworn way of life and a new one struggling to be born. At this historic G-Force turning point, we are fortunate that the Web is available to help us reshape our lives.

Peek into any teenager's room and you will glimpse the future. Like today's "screenagers," we all soon will spend more time with our PCs than our TVs. The digital pathway streaming into our homes will be "live" — an always-on "evernet" through which we communicate with the world as we conduct every aspect of a home-based, cyber-spaced life.

The Web provides a new "life stream" and a new "social glue" that will re-bond our families, rebuild our communities, renew our personal and national security, and restore our prosperity.

HOW FUTURISTIC IS YOUR FAMILY?

Futuristic families, looking forward eagerly and with confidence, will readily and quickly change their life plans. They will manage and benefit from the G-Forces of change to "future-proof" their lives by adopting a "Web Lifestyle."

But how futuristic is your family? How digital is your household? How many TVs, PCs, cellphones, and PDAs are in your household?

How active are you online? How many years have you been online? How many websites are on your "favorites" list? How many hours per day are all family members online? How many names are there in your e-mail address book? How many e-mails are sent daily from home? How many times per month do you buy online? How many family members telecommute, at least some of the time?

What other things do you do online? To what extent do you manage your household appointment calendar and family schedules online? Bank online? Go online for education or school purposes? Go online for healthcare needs? Go online for family entertainment purposes? Go online for spiritual needs? Go online for civic or political purposes? Operate a business online?

This book will help you answer these questions. But if you wish to assess in more detail how well your family is prepared for and is adopting a Web Lifestyle, you can go to the website www.Future-Trends.com where you will find a series of quiz questions and worksheets to help you figure it out.

The "Web Lifestyle"

So, what is a "Web Lifestyle" and how will we live it?

Bill Gates, the chairman of Microsoft, predicted in 1997 that the majority of North Americans would be living a Web Lifestyle within a decade. That means by 2007 at the latest. There is no reason to doubt his prediction. After all, Microsoft is investing billions of dollars a year to make this way of life possible. But can it all happen so quickly?

There's a real tendency to *over*estimate how much things will change in the near term (causing, for example, the 2000 stock market "bubble"). But we also tend to *under*estimate how much things will change over a decade. And many are vastly underestimating the Web and the enormous changes it will bring to our lives.

To find out how much our daily lives will change, let's briefly visit a year-2010 family.

LIFE IN 2010

It's morning in cyber-America 2010, and a Wichita family is preparing for the day.

Mom asks her always-on, six-foot-square WebWall to display the family's global investment portfolio based on overnight price changes in foreign markets. Then she asks it to show her and her husband's custom e-news top stories.

Then, preparing for a short drive to a working lunch with a new client, she uses a card-sized WebPhone with an e-paper, scroll-out screen to call up a mapping program. Linked to a satellite hovering above the earth, it will guide her to the exact location of the company she is to visit.

Once in her electric WebMobile, she'll download real-time traffic data so the self-driving car can take the easiest route. Before leaving, she zaps a weekly cyber-cash allowance to each kid's WebPhone and also asks it to find Brazilian suppliers her client might need, then to send that info to her car before she arrives there.

Dad instructs his WebTablet: "Dial Mr. Fuji at Ford Asia. He'll be in the Air China lounge at Tokyo airport." Mr. Fuji's mobile WebPhone number pops onto his scroll-out screen along with Ford Asia's homepage in a window.

Within seconds, Mr. Fuji's face appears in the tele-talk window. He answers "Moshi," which Dad's WebPhone instantly translates to "Hello." Dad says, "Hello Mr. Fuji, how are you?" which the gizmo translates to "Konnichi wa, Fuji-san, ogenki desu ka?" And so it goes, each speaking their own language as the gadgets simultaneously translate.

They discuss their planned joint bid to take over Lucky Auto, a Chinese firm. As they talk, Dad asks his computer to bring up Lucky's homepage and a list of news items on the firm since their last chat. They debate their final bid as Mr. Fuji calls up a credit report on Lucky. After further discussion, they agree on an offer Mr. Fuji will present in Beijing. They e-mail a digitally co-signed memo to each other's boss about the final bid and Mr. Fuji dashes for his flight.

Next, Dad asks his WebPhone to read out a list of urgent video-mail messages and, noticing the need to visit a client in Paris, instructs the WebPhone's smart agent to find next Monday's most convenient flight options.

The couple's "screen-age" son keeps his computer on constantly, alert for beeps that signal incoming M3 (multimedia-mail) on exam results and confirmation of acceptance into his next global e-learning course. In fact, most students use M3 and tele-chat to study collaboratively with fellow students around the world in courses monitored by a roster of superstar professors.

Meanwhile, nine-year-old Missy is about to resume presiding over a WebClass for 60 grown-ups who want to learn everything about the Web. Yesterday she told them how she first learned to use the Web in e-kindergarten, later setting up her own personal homepage in "e-grade 2," and making "WebPals" all over the world. Today she'll show them how to assemble their own homepage and how to surf for any topic under the sun. Tomorrow she'll show them how to e-shop.

Grandma, who is in Missy's WebClass, is downloading her vital signs, blood readings, and last night's EKG scan to her physician's mobile office as part of her daily e-medical routine. If attention is required, the doctor will e-mail her to advise what time he will make a house call or to confirm that he has e-mailed a revised prescription to the pharmacy for home delivery within the hour.

Sound far-fetched? Not so! This is not Oz.

Many families, in Kansas and across America, Canada, and many European and other countries, already live at least partially this way. Soon, most of us will be living our lives in even more fantastic ways as networked families.

The Networked Family

Just as TV clearly changed family life, society, commerce, and politics, so will the Web, except in different ways.

The Web extends our personal space well beyond our living

rooms to the entire planet. Your PC is your world. And so the world is yours.

When TV came along, not all family members enjoyed equal stature, whether on program choice or seating arrangements. Dad's love of sports pushed aside the viewing preferences of wife and kids. When dad wasn't home, the kids decided what to watch. Mom was least likely to choose what to watch unless nobody else was home. Sadly, many families are still like that.

It was much the same when the family PC first entered the home, with Internet use initially dominated by men. But then children came into their own and, in 1999, women drew alongside men on a 50–50 basis as online users. Now they're ahead.

As a result, a different set of household rules and family practices are emerging. For example, the social function of keeping up family contacts is gravitating to the Web and is more often than not carried out by women. Women, much more so than men, define themselves through their social relations and so they serve as the communications hub for family, relatives, and friends. In the Web world, the family becomes a network and, as relatives disperse, the Web is their gathering place.

Life Stream

All of us connected to the Web will have our own homepage. It will serve as a mobile, ubiquitous personal portal that, wherever we are, will let us interact with, and immediately focus in on, our "life stream" — all our daily activities and all the data associated with them.

Homepages will replace phone listings. Of course, as with unlisted phone numbers, those who want to drop out of cyber-society simply won't put a homepage online. But homepages and e-mails already are widely used to share year-end letters and to show off wedding and baby photos. Recently even a birth was webcast!

Families are coming together online to celebrate birthdays, catch up on relatives, plan weddings, organize re-unions, or mourn deaths. Their online greetings are slowly turning paper cards into museum curiosities.

You can even get married online. Those wishing to bond forever electronically can invite hundreds and thousands of witnesses to virtually attend the wedding at The First Electronic Church of America. The couple goes online to the wedding ceremony page, fill in their names and hometowns, type in their respective responses, and make their vows. The pastor witnesses and validates the couple's marriage and declares them legally married.

That may not be for everyone. But we will interact through our personal portals for most routine needs. All of our interactions and transactions with everybody in the world will go through our life stream. All our letters, billing records, product manuals, catalogs — everything, will be digitized and made part of our life stream database.

You already can aggregate all your Web affairs onto a single page at Yodlee or CashEdge — e-mail, banking, stocks, book orders, job searches, you name it — wherever you happen to be.

Your confidential and secure homepage will put your entire life online, in date order, searchable from your digital birth certificate onward. This won't be stored in files and folders on your PC. That obsolete, 1950's-era pigeon-holing paradigm will be replaced by an e-scrapbook or e-diary of your life's events that streams across any screen you care to access, using Mirror Worlds Technologies' "Scopeware" or Franklin Covey's "OnePlace" software. It will be a multimedia voice-activated stream where you can call up any "file" or scrap of paper or photo you want, whenever you want it.

Your homepage also will outlive you, making you immortal. Someone long ago set up a Virtual Memorial Garden on the Web where friends and family can display epitaphs and pictures of deceased loved ones. Just as you see photos of ancestors pasted up at Asian family shrines or in Buddhist temples, even the dead will have a homepage bearing testimony to their many living achievements.

And if you really want to live life to the fullest, a personal homepage will be essential to 21st-century freedom and happiness.

The "Intercom" of Life

As explored in detail later in Part I, the Web thus creates a new pathway for life — for work, education, shopping, recreation, and much more. Each family will have the world at its fingertips for children's homework, for cross-border online shopping, for tele-working, for staying in constant touch with friends, relatives, and colleagues, for running a family business, and so on.

And with "always-on" broadband Web access, we will keep our machines running 24 hours a day, giving us a permanent, persistent connection to others. The Web will be the "intercom" of life.

Just as people turn automatically to a radio, TV, or newspaper, millions of us already use the Web daily — often several times a day — to check weather, traffic, news, and sports, to manage our finances, watch stocks, and file our tax returns, to buy flowers, books, music, toys, groceries, clothing, air tickets — even cars. In other words, most of us in North America already use the Web in much the same way that others still use the postal service, the Yellow Pages, the telephone, or go to the bank and go shopping in stores. To them, using a phone, TV, or car, or going shopping is second nature — an integral part of life. We take the Web for granted.

By 2005, most people worldwide will take the Web for granted; they won't even notice it. It will be second nature to turn to the Web for shopping, education, healthcare, entertainment, communication, and to earn a living. Computers will "disappear" in the sense that we now take cars, microwaves, toasters, and phones for granted. Truly useful technologies always become "part of the furniture." Thirty years ago, the idea of a phone in the bedroom was thought ridiculous; today they hang by the toilet — and people surf in bed!

"Blending" to Win Back Time

Surfing families "blend" their lives by managing their own time. In the agricultural era, as noted earlier, people set their own hours. Sure, the cows had to be milked within certain timeframes, and tasks had to be organized around the weather and the seasons. But people managed their own time until the factory came along. You had to get to the factory on time, take fixed breaks, and quit at a certain time. This clock-driven system was perpetuated in the 9–5 office commuting routine. The Web gives us back our time and can bring far more flexibility to our days.

Each day, the average adult spends eight hours sleeping, two hours eating, and one hour grooming, leaving thirteen hours for other stuff. But work takes seven hours plus a two-hour commute, cutting available time to four hours. Of that, one hour is spent shopping, two hours are wasted on TV, leaving but one hour for family and friends.

Savvy families free up at least six hours of extra time. By telecommuting, they avoid a two-hour commute, do seven hours work in six, save half an hour on grooming, and need half an hour less sleep. That alone saves four hours. They also quit watching TV, instead spending those two hours online (not including online work time). In turn, that lets them save half an hour on shopping and similar wait-in-line daily activities.

Overall, time-blending families thus have five hours for family and friends, not just one hour. Better still, because they manage their own time, they are free to decide when to do what and how much time to allocate to each activity. Even if they decide to spend two to three hours a day starting a part-time business, they still have at least twice as much time as before to spend with family and friends. And, in any event, they are in and around the home all day.

At-home families manage their own time and allocate it to various tasks almost on an as-needed or just-in-time basis. They blend all aspects of their lives, multi-tasking their time as the precious resource that it is.

Where are you spending your precious 24 hours? How might you change that for the better? Take time out to think about it!

The New "Social Glue"

Every new technology we bring home — cellphone, answering machine, fax machine, PC — changes how we interact with the outside world. Some fear that "cocooning" at home, particularly Web surfing, isolates people.

It turns out not to be so. Users overwhelmingly say the Web has the exact opposite effect; it helps them improve their connections with their own family, with relatives and friends, and with far-flung colleagues, often rekindling long-lost relationships.

Indeed, heavy Web users say they are far more family-oriented and believe that their families are more intact because they can stay together, work together, play together, and learn together. In these families, work and home have really become intertwined and inextricably linked in a new, blended lifestyle where they grow together, not apart.

It also turns out that the vast majority of users lead more robust social lives than those who shun the Web. They are not lonely or alienated but vibrant socialiizers who devote more time to local civic and community affairs than non-users. In fact, many say the Web helps them better connect with the real world.

As the Web goes mobile, increasingly we will hold the world in the palms of our hands, everywhere we are. The ubiquitous global Web thus becomes the new "social glue" that holds society and families together.

In turn, the more virtually connected we become, distance shrinks but our explorable space expands. That leaves us with only one fixed point of reference — the family home.

Web-Connected Homes

Homes themselves are starting to be networked via what computer people call a "server" — basically a PC that sits in a closet, utility room or basement, like the electricity panel or phone junction box.

This server connects individual rooms, either wirelessly or via wall outlets. It also monitors and controls all multimedia traffic flowing in and out of the home to every appliance in the home. Tomorrow's homes will have "smart," chip-based appliances such as furnaces and air conditioners, plus lighting, security, and lawn sprinkler systems. Chips will be embedded in walls, ceilings, floors, carpets, draperies — all silently monitoring your home.

Empty rooms will adjust perfectly to pre-set temperatures when someone enters them for the first time and again when they leave. Lights and window coverings will adjust automatically at dusk or dawn, at any time of year and according to your geographic location, without needing to be pre-set.

The system will learn the way lights and appliances are connected and how you like to operate them. Then it can replay the same patterns later to make your home more comfortable while you're in it or make it look "lived in" while you're out. If you're going out, you simply tell your home and it immediately turns off all electrical outlets so that you do not accidentally leave on potentially dangerous items such as coffee pots or irons.

Your house also will have multi-scheme lighting where various light combinations achieve different effects. A simple voice command will darken your home-theater, dim other lights for entertaining, brighten kitchen counters, or spotlight artwork.

Standalone wired desktop PCs and wireless portable devices such as PC tablets and WebPhones will communicate via the server. Typical applications will include Web access, telecommuting, distance learning, tele-medicine, video-telephony, appliance management, security systems, power control, automated utility meter reading, electric car recharging and info-downloads, multimedia gaming and entertainment, online shopping, financial services and bill payment, electronic voting — the list goes on.

You will be able to communicate with your digital domicile from your WebPhone wherever you are. On the way home you could call in and tell it to change its control sequence to adjust the heat or air-con, put on your favorite music, fill up the Jacuzzi, or de-activate the security system to let in a specific neighbor or unexpected house guest whose arrival is imminent.

If, while you're out, someone rings your doorbell, your WebPhone could automatically alert you and show you a live picture of who's there. And door handles with built-in fingerprint identifiers will be linked to your home's security system to allow or deny access to the house, garage, or any inside room.

To make all this possible, your home may need to be re-wired — or at least have a wireless network installed. At the end of 2002, only 12 million U.S. homes had some form of digital network installed. Only 20 million had broadband access. But the demand for high-speed Web access will drive the expansion of home networking and bring broad-band to the home, either through souped-up phone wires or coaxial cable and small dish antennas.

In digital homes, as noted, the TV won't be the family focus. Moreover, many tasks now performed on PCs will move to mobile Web tablets or WebPhones. Home theaters with giant screens and surround sound will be commonplace and relatively cheap.

The family room and adjoining kitchen will continue to be the family communications hub. Walk into your kitchen and, with a sim-ple voice command, you can scan your video messages from family and friends on a flat-panel display embedded in the countertop or the fridge door panel. The system will read out loud all your fax, e-mail, phone, and video doorbell messages. You will simply tell the system which ones to save, print, or delete as you go along.

Your smart fridge will be a multimedia communications tool. Apart from organizing your online shopping list (discussed in a later chapter), it will play video clips or let you listen to music or the radio. Family members will use the fridge to compile "to do" lists and the system will maintain a composite family calendar.

Thus everyone will be "on the same page" for every possible life event such as birthdays, scheduled children's sporting events, out-of-town trips, car care, home repair, yard maintenance, bill payment and investing, pet care, medical appointments — the list goes on.

WEB AS SECOND SKIN

We won't be able to gauge the real impact of the Webolution on family life and society for at least 20 years. What has happened already is bound to be very small in comparison to what lies ahead.

For starters, the uptake of the Web is much more rapid than for previous media. As recently as 1970, only 40 percent of North American homes had color TV. At the end of 2001, most families had more than one PC and about 60 percent were online. The 80 percent mark should be reached in 2003, only 10 years after the first Web browser software made it all possible.

By 2005, about 90 percent of homes will be using the Web routinely, many of them several hours a day. Before then, Web usage will surpass TV watching. It's easy to see why 98 percent of households will be online well before 2010.

By then, the Web will be the ubiquitous "dial tone" of everyday life, the rule rather than the exception. Each home will have its own "www" address that will be more widely used than its street address, zip code, and phone number combined.

As the decade draws to a close, the Web undoubtedly will have changed society. Indeed, not to be on the Web will be as absurd as not having running water or electricity. Life will be very different. We'll wonder how we ever got along without the Web.

By then, the Web will be society!

PART I

THE G-FORCES OF CHANGE
Bringing the Web Lifestyle

What do the underlying G-Forces imply for our future? How will our nation, our economy, our high-tech revolution, our political system, our social institutions, our communities change?

What does it all mean for us and our families?

As noted earlier, this book presents two main streams of thought. The long-term social, technical, economic, and political G-Forces are converging to:

1. **Reverse** many ways of doing things, restoring many rich aspects of life that were killed or suppressed by the Industrial Revolution; and

2. **Future-Proof** our society, our families, and our way of life, paving the way for still greater achievements of individual and societal success, via the unfolding Internet Revolution, or "Webolution."

The biggest G-Forces for North America in this decade are:

- **SOCIAL: Regeneration and Ethnicity**
- **TECHNICAL: The Wireless "Webolution" of Life**
- **ECONOMIC: The "Prosumer" Super Boom**
- **POLITICAL: Globalization and e-Democracy**

Each is discussed in separate G-Force chapters in Part I.

SOCIAL G-FORCES
Regeneration and Ethnicity

Two major social G-Forces are at play in North America:

- **a shift to a new generation of people;**
- **a changing ethnic make-up of society.**

Firstly, every society literally regenerates itself with each new generation of people. No generation has precise boundaries but there are birth cycles of about 18 years in length. At present, the relative North American generations are:

- **By-the-Book** (born 1911–1928)
- **By-the-Clock** (born 1929–1945)
- **Baby-Boom** (born 1946–1964)
- **Gen-X** or **Baby-Bust** (born 1965–1982)
- **Gen-Y** or **Web-Gen** (born 1983–2001)

Each generation bears a strong imprint of the era in which it is born and raised. Its values are molded not just by those inherited from parents, as we shall see, but from the defining moments of its era.

Secondly, society is changing dramatically, due to immigration from other than Europe, to become a "globalized" multicultural mosaic.

In turn, these new generations of people are integrating the Internet into their lives, making the Web Lifestyle an inevitable social phenomenon.

GENERATIONAL LIFESTYLE SHIFTS

There are currently five generations of social importance in North America, all born since the onset of World War I. Yes, I know there are many people aged 90 and above. God willing, my mother will soon be one of them. But they are not large enough in number to have any major effect on how society is changing; they have no interest in a Web Lifestyle.

The five lifestyle generations are reviewed below. Obviously, one generation comes to prominence as it gains majority and the previous generation loses social influence. In that "the world's a stage," the new generation parades into the play of life and changes the plot. Society thus literally re-generates itself with new ideas and new sets of values. They create a new lifestyle.

Let's review each of the five generations in turn to see how they might be attuned to a Web Lifestyle.

- **By-the-Book (born 1911–1928)**
  - Telegraph-era great-grandparents;
  - 5% of the population (1% by 2010);
  - Defining moments: World War I, Roaring 1920s, and the Great Depression.

This generation believes history moves in orderly straight lines. Conditioned by the dots and dashes of the Morse code, they dot every "i" and cross every "t".

Highly resistant to change, few of them will ever alter their lifestyle. While most were stunned by 9/11, few will behave any differently; they were stay-home types anyway. Yet, being home bodies, it is unlikely any will ever go online to live any aspect of a Web Lifestyle.

• By-the-Clock (born 1929–1945)

- Radio-era grandparents and great-grandparents;
- 15% of the population (12% by 2010);
- Defining moments: Great Depression,
  World War II and the Cold War.

This generation built the national highway system and drove across it in their Chevrolets. Often obsessed with outmoded habits, few ever used a PC at work; they delegated their e-mail.

Only 15 percent have Web access at home, using it mainly for e-mail, health info, hobbies, news, and weather. Tending to be affluent and well educated, they first go online at the coaxing of their children and grandchildren. Others will not go online until the Web becomes easier to use, if at all. In fact, 56 percent say they'll never go online.

However, the youngest of the group, born after 1940, will be much like Baby Boomers and will embrace a Web Lifestyle.

• Baby-Boom (born 1946–1964)

- TV-era parents and grandparents;
- 30% of the population (28% by 2010);
- Defining moments: Cold War, JFK, Vietnam,
  Moon Landing, Computers, 9/11.

This generation was psychologically "shot" by the JFK, RFK, and Martin Luther King assassinations. Idealistic in the 1960s, they turned pragmatic to end the Vietnam War and were inspired by space exploration and computer developments. But 9/11 stunned them again and they fully support the War on Terrorism.

Though heavily influenced by television, Boomers became computer literate in the workplace, embraced PCs and cellphones, and gravitated naturally online at home. Having restored fiscal responsibility to the nation in the 1990s, only to face the terrorist security threat, Boomers will help lead institutional and family change to preserve the American Dream in the Internet Age.

Almost all of them will live a Web Lifestyle and pursue a cyber version of the American Dream.

• Gen-X or Baby-Bust (born 1965–1982)

- MTV-era children of the Boomers;
- 20% of the population (21% by 2010);
- Defining Moments: Booming 1990s, Internet "Bubble," 9/11 and "War on Terrorism."

Counter-culture to their Boomer parents, Gen-Xers are more self-sufficient and, being less-inclined to pursue a career, are highly entrepreneurial. Having experienced the tech "bubble" (which they helped create) and the terrorism attack of 2001, Gen-X will turn out to be somewhat like the By-the-Clock generation that experienced the Great Depression and World War II.

Fiscally conservative and globally oriented pragmatic managers, in the wake of 9/11 they will aim to restore financial freedom and bring security to their lives and their families.

Being heavy Web users, they will tend to operate online businesses and push for political reform via the Internet. All of them will adopt a Web Lifestyle. Most of them already have!

• Gen-Y or Web-Gen (born 1983–2001)

- PC-era children of the Web;
- 30% of the population (32% by 2010);

• Defining Moments: 9/11 and "War
  on Terrorism" plus Internet II.

This cusp-of-the-millennium generation had no defining moment until 9/11 and it will govern their lives. Nor has Gen-Y known a world without PCs and they surf the Web by instinct. Almost one hundred percent of those aged 12 through 17 use the Web as an educational resource. They also use it as a place to hang out and stay in touch with friends via e-mail and instant messaging.

Endlessly searching for and adopting new ideas, they are techno-pioneers and globally aware. Upbeat and wholesome, for them a globalized Web Lifestyle is the only natural way to live. The eldest of them are now starting their own families; the youngest will do so around the year 2020. Watch out! The world truly will never be the same for Gen-Y — nor for the rest of us when it gains sway.

Each generation, as it ages, gradually attains political maturity and majority, bringing new ideas and values to bear across society. For now, the Baby Boomers hold the societal and political levers. But as they age, the follow-on generations will gradually come to influence and define a new culture.

While 9/11 and the Web affect us all, they will define Gen-Y and most Gen-Xers for the rest of their lives. As these two generations together become the social majority later this decade, their values and beliefs — their culture, their Web way of life — will become the cultural norm for society at large.

Since Gen-X and Gen-Y are the dominant daily users of the Web, they will live a Web Lifestyle without giving it a second thought. And so the Web will become the social norm for all of North America.

Globalized Multiculturalism

Despite many obstacles, North America also is gradually becoming a globalized multicultural society, thanks not only to immigration but to inter-ethnic and inter-faith marriages and their offspring. The Internet also is a potent force for trans-cultural understanding.

Modern nation states are increasingly multicultural and this is an increasingly powerful societal G-Force in North America. By 2050, according to U.S. Census Bureau projections, Hispanics will account for 21 percent of the American population, Blacks 15 percent, and Asians 10 percent, with Whites making up the remaining 53 percent — down from 76 percent in 1990 and 72 percent in 2000.

As for Canada, it is officially bilingual — English and French — but prides itself on its inter-ethnicity. Since 1970, the majority of Canadian immigrants have been "people of color" and the country instituted a multicultural policy in 1971, later passed as the Canadian Multiculturalism Act of 1988. Again due to immigration, this former British colony and once European-dominated society now is a global mosaic. In fact, Chinese now is Canada's third most-spoken mother tongue.

The coming North American multicultural society occurs naturally due to higher birth rates amongst some minorities and high levels of immigration, especially in recent years. Inter-ethnic marriage also naturally increases due to immigration, especially among subsequent-generation minority immigrants, many of whom come from countries with mixed-marriage traditions.

The rates of inter-marriage among many immigrant minorities now rival those of second-generation European immigrants whose parents came to North America a century ago. And inter-marriage among those descendents, over time, all but erased ethnic stereo-types that once categorized white people. Indeed, by 1990, only about 20 percent of white couples shared the same ethnic heritage. Such trends are a harbinger of what life in broader society will be like in the future.

That said, Asians are the greatest users of the Internet — well ahead of Caucasians — and Hispanics are catching up fast, as are African-Americans.

In short, the Web is going mainstream. And all ethnic groups will play a full role in bringing the Web Lifestyle to fruition across North America.

TECHNICAL G-FORCES
Wireless "Webolution" of Life

The overwhelming technology G-Force is the Internet Revolution — the "Webolution."

Building for three decades, powered by the mighty microchip, before the Webolution ends it will dwarf the Industrial Revolution and reverse much of what that put in place.

Despite the tech-stock "bubble" and dot-com shake-out of 2000, the Internet juggernaut rolls on inexorably and will dominate the future.

The Internet isn't dead; it has passed from its initial hype to its realism phase and is about to gain a critical mass of users that will bring it to the forefront again — this time as part of our lives.

We are fast approaching what scientists call a "tipping point" or "inflection point" where networked information will become instantaneously available to at least a billion people.

As this occurs, around 2005, the Web will have become an everyday fact of life for a majority of North Americans.

The Web has not gasped its last breath. It's growing at breathtaking speed and becoming as essential as breathing!

The majority of us will be living a Web Lifestyle faster than most of us realize or expect.

Driven by Microchips

The Webolution all began with the microchip. Built into computers, cellphones, and other appliances that drive the Webolution, chips were invented in 1971 by Intel. Ever since, driven by Moore's Law (named after Intel co-founder Gordon Moore), chips have doubled their performance, at lower cost, at least every 18 months. No other technology has ever come close to doing so.

By 1980 a single chip had 6,000 tiny transistor circuits etched into its surface — transistors that cost a dollar apiece. Today's chips have 50 million transistors squeezed onto them and one dollar buys one million transistors.

The first transistorized IBM computer was built in 1954 with only 2,000 transistors. By 1986, a state-of-the-art PC — basically a word-processor that was no more than a glorified typewriter — ran at what then seemed like a super-fast speed of 16 megahertz. Current machines run at 4-gigahertz. In 1991, there were less than a thousand pages of information on a crude Internet. The first Web browser came in 1993. Today, a top-of-the-line PC pulls down millions of pages of information from 3.6 billion websites on the Google search engine in a split second.

And we ain't seen nothing yet. In late 2001, Intel announced the world's fastest silicon transistors that run 1,000 times faster than a Pentium four and are so tiny that 25 as many of them — one billion all together — can be packed onto a single chip. By 2005, a computer chip containing 10 billion transistors will cost less than a potato chip. By 2010, 20-GHz chips — versus today's 4.0-GHz — will have 20 billion transistors. They'll do a trillion instructions per second and perhaps match the ability of the human brain.

Maybe we'll eat them as brain food. Don't laugh! These and still better chips will make simultaneous speech recognition and language translation commonplace. And in 2002, scientists announced a chip smaller than a little fingernail that can be implanted in the body to monitor heart beat, blood sugar, and other vital signs and send data wirelessly to handheld devices or over the Web.

There are scores of chips for every person on earth. By 2010, there will be 30,000 embedded chips for each of us. That's 200 trillion chips, all 10 million times more powerful than today's.

Thanks to these astonishing advances, the cost-effectiveness of computers improved 100 million-fold from 1958 to 1997 — they were 100,000-fold more powerful but their cost dropped 1,000-fold. By 2010, PCs will be 100 million times more powerful again. And everybody in North America will have at least one!

Today, a brand-new PC is switched on for the first time in human history every second, 24 hours a day non-stop around the world. In 1993, there were only 5,000 computers connected to the Internet; by 2000, more than 240 million PCs were connected. In November 2000, 407 million people were online worldwide and that zoomed to 513 million by August 2001. Today it is 620 million. By 2010, at least two billion will be online, often via cellphone.

There are more cellphones sold every year than PCs — two per second around the clock — and the newest ones are permanently connected to the Web. It is estimated that by 2004 there will be one billion cellphones, half of them permanently online "WebPhones."

Awesome Wealth-Creating Potential

With this awesome computing power at our disposal, the enormous web of wealth that will flow from it is unimaginable. No set of technologies ever in history has seen anywhere near such improvements in its productivity and efficiency. The closest are textile machines and steam engines that drove the Industrial Revolution.

Productivity is the key to better living standards. And it sped up sharply in the late 1990s to double that of the prior two decades. Annual productivity gains were still running at a 2.7 percent clip, even during the 2001 economic slowdown. Furthermore, experts say Moore's Law has at least 10 years still to run and will drive the Webolution across all societies, turning the world on its head.

The Internet also is entering our lives faster than any previous medium. To reach 50 million North American users, radio took 38 years and TV took 13 years. The Web reached 50 million people in only five years. Moreover, usage is growing five times faster than TV and ten times faster than radio. About 60 percent of households already have a PC and are online. Many are still learning the benefits of the Web and few would yet claim to live a Web Lifestyle. But that will happen fast as people gain online experience.

Internet Hype and Reality

What's the hype and reality of all this? After all, until 9/11, the Web was blamed for North America's economic downturn in 2000–2001. When the "bubble" burst in 2000, the Web was seen as the "Silly.Con Valley Folly." Dot-coms became dot-bombs, tens of thousands of people lost their jobs, and many lost money on collapsed tech company stocks. It became conventional wisdom to blame technology for these losses and national troubles.

The reality is quite different. The impact of the money and job losses is vastly exaggerated. A recent study by the Pew Internet & American Life Project found that only seven percent of U.S. families lost money on a dot-com stock and only nine percent of Americans say they know someone laid-off by a dot-com. Only 30 percent of U.S. adults have even followed dot-com developments.

By contrast, the Web continues to seep into our everyday lives. Just consider the following inescapable facts:

- Every second, even in 2000 and 2001, a brand-new PC is switched on for the first time in history.
- Every second, somebody goes online for the first time.
- Internet traffic in 2001 quadrupled over that of 2000.
- Users spent 20 percent more time online in 2001 over 2000.
- Every four seconds, AOL gains a new subscriber.
- AOL members average 70 minutes a day online.
- About five million people are online at any given moment.
- Every five seconds, another product is sold online.
- Every seven seconds, somebody new shops online.
- Online sales in 2000 doubled over 1999, and almost doubled again in both 2001 and 2002.

All this is happening *despite* the dot-com shake-out, the economic slump, terrorist attacks, and the War on Terrorism. Users continue to log on — as if none of these things ever happened — to search, e-mail, chat, telecommute, shop, bank, download music, worship, do homework, start an e-business, and so on, in ever-growing numbers.

The Web has become an accepted medium. People are not going to stop using it any more than they will toss out their PCs and cellphones or rip out their telephones. There are three million digital switches for everyone on Earth, a PC for every 12 people, a cellphone for every six. None of these are going away, other than to be replaced by even more fantastic devices that change the world and our lives yet again.

Yet many media pundits, business people, and politicians chose to ignore or pooh-pooh this ongoing Webolution. In truth, we had a "bubble" precisely because people know that the Web is the future and want to get in on it — which they are still doing, in droves!

Unfounded Skepticism

Such ignorance is not new. Every new technology meets denial. Skeptics often raise one or more objections, such as: "It will never work," or "There's nothing new about it," or "Nobody needs it." Indeed, nobody watched TV at first. And people once wondered why anybody would ever want a phone in their car. These quotes are well known but still amusing:

> This "telephone" has too many shortcomings to be seriously considered as a means of communication. The device is inherently of no value to us.
> —*Western Union Telegraph company memo, 1876*

> Television will never be a serious competitor for radio because people must sit and keep their eyes glued on a screen; the average family hasn't time for it.
> — *New York Times article, 1939*

> There's no reason for anybody to have a computer at home.
> —*Ken Olsen, chair, Digital Equipment Corp., 1977*

Many do not grasp the profundity of the Webolution thus far — never mind where it is inescapably leading. They see the Web as merely another level of technology. They show no foresight as to the inevitable network effect of a wireless, broadband, always-on, multimedia, hyper-speed Web — a "HyperWeb" — on society. More than 60 percent of new broadband subscribers are family residences, not businesses. In fact, broadband is being adopted faster than was TV.

Against this background, Web skeptics are akin to the plodding ploughman who couldn't see how the first steam engine chugging past his field was about to change the world. Their eyes are transfixed by the linear furrows of an old way of life that will soon be washed away by a HyperWeb dramatically different than even today's wonderment.

The Web is in its infancy; a baby barely crawling, never mind toddling, walking, or running, and that will live one hundred years. We've barely seen one percent of it. What emerges will be gigantic. The Webolution is far too big to go *poof*.

WebPhones and WebMobiles

The Web extends all our faculties, becoming our eyes, ears, nose, mouth, hands, and feet. As everything gets connected, the always-on Web will envelop us in a multimedia "info-sphere" that will accompany us everywhere. As McLuhan again saw:

> The electric age ... establishes a global network that has much of the character of our central nervous system; it constitutes a single unified field of experience.

Wherever you go, surrounded by your personal info-sphere, you will be able to talk and walk, listen and watch, compute and surf — and chew gum! — all at the same time. Every day 150,000 people buy a Web-ready cellphone, or WebPhone, and they are now so popular that phone companies are ripping out payphones. Your WebPhone puts the world in your pocket and serves as a personal portal — a genie that's always awaiting your next command. With a WebPhone, you won't click from page to page but will invoke constantly updated, customized content to be always in your presence.

Content will be tele-present in eyeglasses — their transparent, tiny EGD (eye-glass display) appearing as big and as vivid as a 17-inch desktop monitor — as well as in wristwatches, lapel pins and brooches, tiny hearing aids, belts, and other accessories. Indeed, your WebPhone accessories will be discreet fashion statements that identify you as a Web Lifestyle *savant*.

Web Lifestyles will be lived out in the car as much as on a PC or a WebPhone. There are more than 220 million cars in North America and their owners collectively spend 100 million hours a day in them. The car will be a big part of the mobile Web Lifestyle. People use their cars in many info-intensive ways. The radio and tape deck or CD player tend to be in constant use. The cellphone — which 99 percent of people once said they would never want in a car — is commonplace, and new cars come with built-in, voice-activated cellphones. Mobile workers even set up makeshift offices in their cars, either on the passenger seat in sedans or at a table and swivel chair in minivans. In short, as I told a conference of automobile engineers in 1994, the car is an "information appliance."

The car in the Internet era is a medium: a computerized content carriage. By 2004, Internet connectivity in cars will be available to anyone who wants it, either through built-in appliances or through a portable WebPhone. More and more, cars will be a networked and permanent part of the Web Lifestyle.

It won't be long before traffic cops hear the lame excuse, "Sorry officer, I was just surfing."

With more than 600 million people already online, the Web-olution is gaining mass adherents. It offers something familiar yet so dramatically improved that millions of people are embracing it *en masse*.

Like the Industrial Revolution, the Web is not just technology; it brings a brand new socio-economic system. A massive network that mirrors society, the Web is about people, family, and community. Together, the changes it brings will totally restructure the family in the most positive and exciting way for the future. The ongoing response by Web Lifestyle families will determine our collective future.

ECONOMIC G-FORCES
"Prosumer"-Driven
Super Boom to 2020

Economics is full of booms and busts — and we're heading into a "Super Boom." Recession and revival is an endless G-Force over a 57.5-year MegaCycle.

The 2000–2001 slowdown was an on-schedule transition in an ongoing boom. As we recover from the tech shake-out and the terrorist attack, the economy will continue its Super Boom growth phase. There will be another slowdown around 2010 before the boom continues to about 2020.

This prosperity phase began in 1993, driven by the high-tech Webolution and now by a new and fast-growing "prosumer" economy.

Future wealth will be created less by major companies and more by a new wave of home-based online entrepreneurs, or "Webpreneurs" — individuals and families who own and operate prosumer e-businesses.

Prosumers both produce and consume their own products and services, selling to themselves and other prosumers through Web-based "network marketing" programs.

By 2010, there might be a billion such prosumer e-businesses — the "Web Billion."

The 57.5-Year MegaCycle of Prosperity

A Russian economist, Nikolai Kondratieff, long ago described a long-wave cycle of about 60 years. Based on my own 30+ years of research while in the banking industry and since, I believe this cycle averages 57.5 years. This MegaCycle has rising and subsequent falling trends, each lasting just shy of 29 years.

The Kondratieff wave also was studied by Harvard economist Joseph Schumpeter in conjunction with other short and medium business cycles. He argued that if cycles of varying lengths exist, then they occur at the same time, compounding each other's effects.

Schumpeter thus aggregated all known short and medium cycles with the Kondratieff Wave. This revealed an undulating long wave similar to what I call the MegaCycle.

The MegaCycle is shown as a thick wiggly line in the chart opposite, taken from my 1989 book G-Forces. The chart has no particular scale; it shows the order of magnitude of fluctuations over time.

The MegaCycle rises and falls in six installments — three up and three down — that average about 115 months. This 9.5-year interval matches the Juglar Cycle (identified by French economist Clément Juglar) drawn from 160 years of data. We thus can rely on the MegaCycle's predictive ability, give or take a month or so.

When the Juglar Cycle falls, the MegaCycle (long wiggly line) dips below the Kondratieff long-wave (smooth line), predicting a recession. Without exception, the recessions that occurred in North America during the current long-wave coincide with the MegaCycle. In other words, economic experience validates it.

Usually, but not always, recessions come immediately *after* the

THE 57.5-YEAR MEGACYCLE

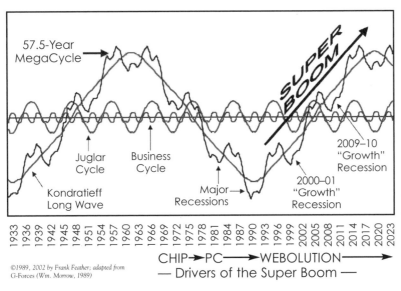

©1989, 2002 by Frank Feather; adapted from
G-Forces (Wm. Morrow, 1989)

CHIP➤PC➤WEBOLUTION➤
— Drivers of the Super Boom —

year in which the short and medium cycles fall together (for instance, after 1961, 1970, 1980, 1989, and 1999). The economy declines most severely when the MegaCycle is at its lowest ebb. The trough of the MegaCycle is marked by two severe recessions — as in 1981–82 and then in 1991–92, which coincided with the Gulf War.

The Super Boom that started in 1993 will continue for two decades to around 2020. As predicted by the MegaCycle, we experienced a "growth" recession in 2000–1, again accompanied by war. "Growth" recessions occur during the Super Boom phase and are much less severe than recessions during the MegaCycle's declining phase. Another will occur around 2009–10, perhaps also accompanied by yet another war. Then I expect the economy to top out around 2020, as it did in 1962–63, exactly 57.5 years previously.

Causes of Boom and Bust

What causes these long-wave boom and bust cycles? The short answer is new generations of people and technology — the social and technical G-Forces discussed earlier.

After the Great Depression of the 1930s and World War II, for example, the economy rebounded thanks to these two primary factors. First, the formation of new post-war families brought the Baby Boom, with births peaking in 1957. Second, factory automation and the build-out of the continental highway system brought goods to market more efficiently. The highways also allowed people to travel, spurring rapid growth in the automobile and travel industries in the 1950s and early 1960s.

Then, lacking major technological innovation until after the microchip's invention in 1971, and hampered by the Vietnam War and two oil-price shocks, the economy gradually ran out of steam.

History shows that most innovation occurs during the economic slump as people frantically seek better ways of doing things. But innovations do not yield economic benefits until as much as 20 years later. It often takes that long to develop applicable products and bring them to market.

Thus the microchip of 1971 and the PC of 1980 didn't start to pay off until the 1990s. The Internet became public in the mid-1990s but the Webolution will only achieve its maximum economic effect during its next 20 years of global expansion, driving the Super Boom forward to at least 2020.

The "Bubble" Explained

Now, skeptics hark back to the Internet "bubble." So before exploring the Super Boom and the prosumer economy, we need to understand why and how the bubble burst in 2000.

Let's first be clear that the bursting of the tech stock bubble did *not* have a lot to do with the dot-com shakeout *per se*. It was a technology mania that became totally irrational and spread across all stock markets, not just the tech-laden Nasdaq.

People overestimated how quickly the Internet would change business in the short term and they drove stocks of all kinds — not just tech stocks — to ridiculously high prices. When the Nasdaq index was at 3000, I warned audiences that it was way ahead of itself, too high, would inevitably correct, and that the higher it went the farther it would fall. This is precisely what happened. After zooming to 5000, it then went too far the other way, well below the 2000 level.

But much of the stock mania had nothing to do with the Internet at all. Indeed, many solid-but-stodgy Dow-listed stocks, such as Coca Cola and Gillette, also were trading at ridiculously high price multiples. And the price of almost *any* tech stock was driven sky-high.

I recall Microsoft CEO Steve Balmer saying publicly that his company's stock was overvalued in 1999 — months before the Nasdaq peaked in March 2000. Amazon's Jeff Bezos actually went on TV warning people *not* to buy the company's clearly overvalued stock.

In fact, the stock market meltdown of 2000 had three main elements, as follows:

1. **Y2K Hangover:** There was bound to be a tech slowdown after the Y2K problem was solved. In the run-

down to December 31, 1999, companies strived frantically to ensure their computer systems would not crash when the clock ticked over to the year 2000. In the end, instead of trying to fix their software, lots of companies simply threw in the towel and bought brand new software and Y2K-compliant hardware. That drove the sales of everything, from software to computers, servers, routers, phone switches — you name it. In turn, that drove profits and share prices. But then, after January 1, 2000, most companies stopped buying all those things and vendor sales peaked out. And it will be well into 2003 before most companies again feel it necessary to upgrade their systems.

2. **Dot-Com Craze:** New start-ups, not even half of them in e-tailing, were making initial public offerings (IPOs) of stock at inflated prices that investors drove to astronomical levels on the first day of trading. Their "executives," who'd never run any business before, became instant multimillionaires. As in any previous entrepreneurial "gold rush," most of these companies became dot-bombs, but not until they too had bought all kinds of technology from manufacturers, in turn driving tech company values to even more unsustainable levels. Then, as the gold rush peaked and dot-coms foundered, those technology sales stopped. Moreover, lots of barely used second-hand equipment was thrown onto the market, again causing tech makers' order books to dry up.

3. **Telecom Scramble:** There also was a mad scramble to build out telephone, cable, and fiber-optic broadband networks worldwide. At one time it seemed as if all major players, plus many heavily indebted start-up telecom firms, were building global broadband networks that inevitably must lead to an over-supply. That's exactly what happened. All told, about 42 million miles of fiber-optic cable — enough to circle the earth 1,600 times! — costing some $95 billion, was laid in the U.S.A. alone between 1997 and 2000. And yet it is estimated that less than three percent of the available capacity was actually being used at the end of 2001. This frenzy put the network builders in heavy debt, with few customers, and left telecom equipment makers with empty order books. So the entire telecom sector saw its stock values plunge, and the most debt-laden firms will not survive. The only "plus" in all this is that we will get access to very cheap bandwidth earlier than was expected. But for the frenzy, the investment in bandwidth would not have been made for another decade.

Clearly, then, the dot-com shakeout was but one part of the bubble and the stock sell-off was long overdue, inevitable, salutary, and healthy. It weeded out the excesses and the weaklings.

The economy is already recovering from the shake-out and 9/11, sending the MegaCycle into the next two decade-long Super Boom growth phases. The Webolution has barely begun.

The New Prosumer Economy

Moreover, the fast-growing wave of prosumer Webpreneur activity will expand the economy through the network effect. Sure, there are limits to how much we can consume. But the buy-direct, do-it-yourself, sell-to-yourself prosumer economy creates tremendous efficiencies. It eliminates costly middlemen, warehouses, and retail distribution. In turn, this will create more net wealth, boosting economic growth at above-average rates.

The new Internet economy is as different as was the old industrial economy from that of the agricultural era. The old factory-centric, product-push, mass production, mass consumption, mass marketing, mass advertising economy is utterly obsolete. The Web blows it to bits.

The Web launches us into a new buyer-centric, product-pull, networked, mass-customized, one-to-one prosumer economy. The Web boosts economic value, to the benefit of both producer *and* consumer. The consumer becomes the producer — what Alvin Toffler in *Third Wave* called the prosumer — of value and wealth.

Prosumerism stems from the self-serve and do-it-yourself movements. They started with self-serve supermarkets, then spread to gas pumps and automated banking machines, and culminated in the growth of do-it-yourself activities such as home renovation.

The old second-wave, *pre*-Web, product-driven company increased shareholder value by extracting it *from* laborers and customers. The new third-wave, *post*-Web, customer-driven enterprise sees customers as complementary, with value to be extracted from entrepreneurial or intellectual capital in the service *of* customers.

Enterprises that focus on lifetime customer value — which Web-enabled one-to-one marketing now permits — see customers as *assets* from which they generate ongoing revenue streams and drive further asset growth.

Prosumers buy from themselves and directly from other prosumers, not from product manufacturers. As the buy-direct prosumerism trend builds, it will de-marketize large portions of various economic sectors and will become an ever-larger part of the economy.

The biggest global movement in this direction is the exploding network or multi-level marketing (MLM) industry. These global entrepreneurs of prosumerism are leading the way in building a meta-market industry that could become the planet's largest industrial sector within a few decades. And they are now doing it over the Internet.

This economic shift is based on the "word-of-modem" network effect that leads prosumers to send friends to their favorite websites. That personal endorsement process has created massive online brand names such as AOL, Amazon, eBay, and Quixtar.

Such companies will leverage the network effect of the Web to capture an ever-increasing market share, built at lower cost, to yield higher profits and/or faster growth.

Each of these are prosumer e-businesses — successful dot-coms — that will "Webolutionize" economics and help drive the economy during its next Super Boom phase to 2010 or so. In turn, this G-Force trend will make the Web Lifestyle an affluent one, especially for those who start their own online prosumer business.

POLITICAL G-FORCES
Globalization and e-Democracy

T he political pendulum always swings in parallel with the other G-Forces of change.

In terms of social change, as a new generation of voters comes to power, they bring different values to the political process, often causing a shift in party allegiance.

The state of the economy also is a major factor in deciding electoral outcomes. When the economy is going well, people are less inclined to bother voting and/or tend not to "rock the boat" by changing the government, and *vice versa.*

In the future, however, technology also will play a large role. Elections will inexorably shift over time to online voting via the Web from home. The Internet also will facilitate the emergence of a more participatory democracy, or "partocracy."

The biggest political G-Force is geo-political. The trend towards globalization and the "War on Terrorism" could evolve into a highly dangerous "Web War." This seriously threatens our very way of life, in turn calling for urgent action that could greatly influence domestic election outcomes.

The solution is to use the Web to future-proof our lives so we can preserve and enhance all of our freedoms.

The Next U.S. President

Generationally speaking, George Bush senior was the last "By-the-Clock" president. Bill Clinton and George Bush junior are the first Baby Boom presidents.

However, later this decade, when the majority of Americans will be online and the Boomers will start to feel their collective mortality, the socio-political pendulum will start to swing yet again. Bush could well be the last Boomer president, with a Gen-X president likely coming to office, perhaps as early as 2004, more likely in 2008, but almost certainly in 2012.

Whenever it happens, as Gen-X and Gen-Y gradually gain power — they will be 53 percent of the population by 2010 — they will be strong family guardians, no-nonsense business managers, spiritual anchors, and the protectors of new social and political values. Society will enter a new era and emerge with entirely new attitudes about family, community, business, economics, politics, world affairs, and domestic life.

The economic G-Forces, as we've seen, point to another Super Boom decade of uninterrupted prosperity until another temporary slowdown around 2010.

In that event, Bush should be re-elected in 2004 and there's a good chance that another Republican will follow him into the White House in 2008. However, as the economy slows around 2010, there likely will be a popular swing back to the Democrats in 2012 for sure. Alternatively, a third-party or independent candidate could easily win.

Much will depend on whether the Bush Administration can balance its books in the aftermath of 9/11. The need to fight the War on Terrorism could drain the treasury and return us to Reagan-era deficits — and then some.

If deficits pile up again, then a Democrat could breeze back into the White House rather quickly. Newly pragmatic Baby Boomers and Gen-Xers want to win the terrorism war we face. But they will not tolerate a return to fiscal recklessness.

Nor will Boomers, Gen-X or Gen-Y continue to tolerate non-participatory democracy. Reform-minded voters came out in unprecedented numbers for John McCain in his 2000 presidential bid and they made Jesse Ventura the Governor of Minnesota.

Even after the passage of the campaign finance reform bill in early 2002, we will see ongoing demands for further campaign finance and electoral reform, leading to experiments in electronic voting and then e-voting from home on Election Day.

Whichever of the two major parties pushes these issues farthest will garner major electoral support. If both fail to do so, then a third party could easily scoop up the votes and sweep into office.

The entire topic of domestic political reform is explored at length later in this book.

The Globalization Genie

On the geo-political front, the signs of major change are already evident. As at other major turning points, political leaders such as Bush and Blair — like Roosevelt and Churchill before them — described the global threat in broad, big-picture terms, communicating freely, and expressing determination to overcome adversity and destroy rather than contain the "evildoers."

As well, people everywhere are focused on the security and well-being of their families and are much more considerate of others. In society at large, individual rights are generally and willingly being subsumed to national interests.

In addition, mobility across national borders is subject to greater security, and immigration is being tightened up, if not put on hold. Indeed, the governments of the U.S., Mexico, and Canada are seeking ways to implement a continent-encompassing, perimeter border like that around Europe. Going beyond its NAFTA free trade pact, what in the future we might call "Amexicana" is slowly integrating politically in the face of globalization.

All nations move from dependence, to independence, and then to regional and global interdependence. The inexorable trend toward globalization is a major G-Force not just of world affairs but of domestic politics. And our network age reflects this evolving reality.

The Cold War divided the world into geo-political camps around issues of national and superpower interests (many of which still exist, by the way). Nevertheless, in contrast to the Cold War, the War on Terrorism is leading us — aided by the G-Forces of a spreading Internet and of economic integration through trade — into the politics of globalization.

Let's consider what British prime minister Tony Blair said about globalization in the aftermath of 9/11.

> I realize why people protest against globalization. We watch aspects of it with trepidation. We feel powerless, as if we were now pushed to and fro by forces far beyond our control. But there's a risk that political leaders, faced with street demonstrations, pander to the argument rather than answer it.

The demonstrators are right to say there's injustice, poverty, environmental degradation. But globalization is a fact and, by and large, driven by people. Not just in finance, but in communication, in technology, increasingly in culture, in recreation. In the world of the Internet, information technology and TV, there will be globalization. And in trade, the problem is not there's too much of it; on the contrary there's too little of it.

The issue is not how to stop globalization. The issue is how we use the power of community to combine it with justice. If globalization works only for the benefit of the few, then it will fail and will deserve to fail.

But if we follow the principles that have served us so well — and make those the guiding light for the global economy — then it will be a force for good and an international movement that we should take pride in leading. The alternative to globalization is isolation.

This is an extraordinary moment for progressive politics. Our values are the right ones for this age: the power of community, solidarity, the collective ability to further individual interests.

As Blair clearly spelled out, we are already global. In fact, we became global in 1969 when we went to the Moon and looked back at Earth to see "the globe" for the very first time.

Globalization cannot be rolled back; it is another genie that escaped its bottle. Those that oppose globalization are opposing the inevitable.

Americanized Globalism

The problem is that many do not understand the true nature of globalization, often seeing it as "Americanization." Even the non-terrorist opponents of globalization — such as the wackos who wreak carnage at IMF and G7 meetings — see it as Americanization.

Having been colonized at least once, many in developing nations fear another version of it, or at least they fear being homogenized. The natural reaction has been what McLuhan called "global retribalization." Ethnic groups are striving to hold on to their cultural roots and often campaigning for their own nation state or resorting to subversion or terrorism.

A whole clutch of new nations was created in the 1950s and 1960s as former colonies gained independence from declining empires. Another clutch was hatched in the 1990s as the Soviet Union morphed into the Commonwealth of Independent States.

Paradoxically, however, thanks to Internet-induced globalization, newly independent nations immediately find they are interdependent. Their false, nationalistic pride thus impedes globalization while misguided terrorism seeks to stop it.

"Glocal" Politics

Globalization and the Web strengthen universal links between people. The Web connects and collects people into groups with shared interests, both globally and locally — it is "glocal." It expands our social world to faraway people yet binds us to our local communities and our homes.

This "glocalization" process overlays both the problems and opportunities of globalization.

And therein lies the major challenge.

In forging healthy and much-needed allegiances to other ethnic, religious, and cultural subgroups, many people also weaken their links with their own nation state. The world thus is reorganizing itself into a series of sub-networks — some of which owe allegiance only to themselves. This runs the risk of undermining each nation's security as well as that of the community of civilized nations as a whole.

At the same time, national governments inevitably find themselves pulled in different directions. It has been clear for at least two decades — since the word "global" first became cliché and the G-Force of globalization gathered strength — that national governments must raise their sights to their global responsibility for security, trade, and general socio-economic integration.

Conversely, their citizens at the local level are scrambling for regional autonomy and greater participation in the political process. To the ancient Greeks, politics meant the involvement and participation of the individual citizen in a world larger than his or her own life or own small circle of family and friends.

Politics thus again becomes both global *and* local, or glocal — just like the Web — as well as individual.

And so now we are joined by the urgent need for mutual global, local, and personal security. Otherwise, the network of global terrorism — which mostly stands opposed to every social, technical, economic, and political G-Force of globalization — could, without any exaggeration, easily erupt into a full-scale war of many dimensions.

The Coming "Web War"

The War on Terrorism is a new world war that could destroy us all.

Just as the world regenerates itself with each new generation of people and technology, so do conflict and the ways of war. We always have to stay several steps ahead of the hackers, the crooks, and the madmen. So the next generation of war likely will be a "Web War" fought against cyber-terrorism.

The last generation of war was the kind fought in Kosovo, then in Afghanistan, and most recently in Iraq. It was based on vastly superior intelligence, advanced information technology, and super-smart weapons. Such wars probably will need to be fought again, with even smarter systems of destruction.

That does not mean, by the way, that we necessarily need the proposed missile-defense shield — the revived Reagan-era "Star Wars" strategy. There will not be a global nuclear war. The Star Wars idea is just a defense industry boondoggle. It is a perfect expression of defensive isolationism and left-brain thinking. It might work and it may protect us from the odd missile that might come from a rogue state, but it can only be a short-term solution to achieving any kind of lasting global peace. We need to defang rogue states such that the missile threat — nuclear or otherwise — remains contained.

This Web War actually has been underway since the so-called but mythical end of the Cold War. In reality, the Cold War became a "Hot War" fought over "cool" media. And now that medium of war is the Web. As the War on Terrorism proceeds, it will end up being fought over the Internet.

Fortunately for peace-loving people everywhere, the Pentagon's Defense Advanced Research Projects Agency (DARPA) — one of the creators of the original Internet — is pushing the development of smart software agents using the latest XML coding that will help us win the Web War, whether it's fought geographically or over the Internet. DARPA wants these systems for command-and-control operations over a "networked network" of information. To that end, a team of global organizations in the Western alliance is working on a top-secret "coalition of agents" project.

To help that project go forward, one of the best things that we ordinary citizens can do is to help spread the Internet across our daily lives by living the Web Lifestyle. Here's why.

The Web War is an info-intensive battle against rogue nations, subversive groups, and individual madmen that aim to subvert Western minds. Cyber-terrorists will try to disrupt, damage, or modify how we think — and our very way of life — via 24-hour satellite TV bombardment and over the Internet. And we must fight them back through the same multimedia channels.

For example, during the war in Afghanistan against Al-Qaeda, we saw how the Qatar-based Al-Jazeera satellite station broadcast non-stop propaganda, including the notorious Osama bin-Laden videotapes. A similar station, Al-Manar, operates out of Lebanon. The mouthpiece of the Hizbullah terrorist group, it promotes and provokes *Jihad* ("holy war") among Palestinians against Israel. It also terrorizes Israelis with shrieking messages that vow the destruction of the "Zionist entity."

The head of Al-Manar plainly states that "Al-Manar is an important weapon for us: a political weapon, social weapon, and cultural weapon." He openly admits the station is "funded by investors whose motivation is political and religious."

Clearly, these so-called "investors" are backers and supporters of global terrorism and aim to attack us through propaganda and psychological warfare. In fact, the head of Al-Manar also admits that it aims "to destroy" its enemies. Could anything be clearer?

Hijacking Our Minds

These and other enemies of "glocalizing" civilization are trying to change what we know — or think we know — about ourselves and our world, without our even being aware of it. They focus on elite and mass public opinion alike and try to modify it to their own ends. They aim to make us destroy ourselves.

Cyber-terrorism will strike directly at our minds, hijacking the way we think and our beliefs, and then using them against us. This would be far more deadly than what took place on 9/11 when a few brainwashed madmen hijacked our own airplanes and flew them into our buildings. The Web War aims to scramble our neurons and fry our brains into capitulation, making previous propaganda campaigns look pathetic by comparison.

Cyber-terrorists will use every means at their disposal: official-looking diplomacy that is far more subversive than a few embassy spies; massive but subtle propaganda and psychological campaigns; opinion deception by infiltrating media; promoting dissent and opposition movements across the Web and in our own local communities.

They won't need to do it by smuggling "sleeper" terrorists past the immigration process. And this is nothing like a few pesky hackers trying to breach computer security for their own self-satisfaction. Nor will they be madmen trained in Al-Qaeda martial arts camps.

This will be an invisible glocal network of thousands of cyber-trained, cyber-expert cyber-terrorists who have only one aim: to utterly and completely destroy our civilization.

Is the West ready? The Business Software Alliance of information technology experts, by a margin of ten to one, say U.S. government security measures taken so far are "not at all adequate." Hence, with a growing cyber threat looming over us, it is astonishing that people still fret about their online privacy or whether it is safe to vote online — which we will and must do.

Indeed, we need not worry too much about whether these cyber-terrorists could hijack an election. They clearly have much larger aims. And we have no choice but to use the Internet to defeat them.

Future-Proof Lives

Fortunately, North Americans tend to be more futuristic than most. We need to expand our worldview and definition of globalization beyond mere trade to see the global village for the networked glocal society that it is.

We need to understand how various tribes, ethnicities, cultural traditions, beliefs, markets, economies, sciences, technologies, and governments — everything about life — are being interwoven to form a new holistic fabric of planetary society. We must ensure it is a network for good, not evil.

In doing so, with all speed we must "webify" and "future-proof" our own society, in every aspect of our lives — individually and collectively — from our business, political, legal, and military systems, to our families and everything else discussed in this book.

This will be a decisive era of secular change, with old institutional frameworks of various kinds replaced by new, Internet-based networks. In turn, pragmatic management of this period will build social confidence that will spawn an upbeat time of strong institutions, families, and communities.

All this will not be done overnight, but it must be done — quickly and decisively. Only then will we preserve our freedoms.

And an early step is to future-proof our families by adopting some or all of the "Nine Ways of the Web Lifestyle" explained next in Part II.

PART II

The NINE WAYS
of the WEB LIFESTYLE

Having explored the "big picture" future and the major G-Forces at play, we now examine each of the "Nine Ways of the Web Lifestyle" in greater detail:

1. **Telecommute: Escape the Skyscraper!**

2. **Shop Online: Have it Delivered!**

3. **Bank Online: e-Manage Your Money!**

4. **School @ Home: e-Learn a Living!**

5. **Self-Doctor: Heal Thyself @ Home!**

6. **Digitize Your Fun: Download It!**

7. **Cyber Worship: Congregate Online!**

8. **Vote Online: Click the Rascals Out!**

9. **Build e-Wealth: Start an e-Business!**

The chapters in Part II are short. But they are designed to explain the trends already underway in these areas in a straightforward way that is both specific and relevant to family lifestyles.

Each chapter describes how and in what ways people are already using and/or will in the future use the Internet to do these nine things — and hopefully will encourage you and your family to do the same.

1

TELECOMMUTE
Escape the Skyscraper!

How much would you give to escape "commute hell" and not have to show up at your office tower cubicle? Millions of North Americans are doing just that.

Believe it or not, the skyscraper era has ended. Tens of millions of people will never again walk past or into a skyscraper — never mind work there — without apprehension. Moreover, in the Web era, 90 percent of those working downtown just don't need to be there to do their jobs.

After 9/11, many urban planners seriously question high-rise densities and centralized workplaces. In 2001, a vast 120 million square feet of office space was vacated across America. In 2002, U.S. businesses vacated another 108 million square feet. That's the equivalent of one Empire State Building being emptied every week!

There's much talk of dispersing still more work to exurban low-rise campuses — and right into the home. In many small towns there's just as much wheeling and dealing as in a big-city skyscraper. In some towns, some 20 percent of residents now conduct commerce at home.

While skyscrapers obviously won't be quickly replaced by home offices, droves of people almost certainly now will opt to work from home. Already, 38 million North Americans telecommute; another 16 million own home-based businesses. And both totals are growing by about four percent a year. All told, more than 60 percent of the U.S. and Canadian workforce is in remote locations anyway, either at home or on the road.

Rethinking career goals and family priorities, the remaining stunned office workers are stepping back to re-evaluate what they want from their next job — even whether they want a "job" at all.

Working couples are deciding they'd rather have at least one parent at home with the kids. Others want fewer days out of town. Millions will move house — right out of town — in search of a slower pace in a safer place.

Unoccupied Skyscrapers

Why do all those banking, insurance, brokerage, advertising, and media employees in Manhattan have to be there anyway? Why were so many there on 9/11? None of them — not one — needed to be there then, before, or since.

Thousands of work-at-home financial advisors handle investment portfolios, do computer consulting, promote travel destinations, develop advertising campaigns, write magazine and newspaper articles, and build business networks — all without ever visiting an office building of any kind.

Even then, during the average workday, those downtown office cubicles aren't truly occupied very much anyway. They are empty 70 percent of the time — yes, 70 percent of the time — as people take breaks, visit the bathroom, go to the water cooler, have lunch, go shopping, drop in on others to chit-chat, and so on. Count in nights, weekends, and holidays, and the actual occupancy rate of most office towers drops to only 15 percent!

What, if any, is the return on investment of all that concrete, steel, and glass? Certainly, the productivity and value-added enjoyed by the employers who insist on occupying these trophy-address paper-shuffling factories in the sky must be abysmal.

So, we'll let the left-brain architects, urban planners, and city politicians decide whether or how to rebuild the Twin Towers.

We need to rethink and rebuild our professional lives.

The Comical Commute

Commuting to downtown office buildings is the utmost idiocy of the modern age. Consider this typically comical day in the life of the average commuter.

> Arising at an ungodly hour, commuters grab a slice of toast and an instant coffee, and dash out of the home — leaving spouse and kids still asleep in bed — either to a cold car or to stand on a windy street corner waiting for a bus that's still blocks away stuck in traffic.
>
> The car driver, 90 percent of the time traveling alone, eagerly listens to weather and traffic reports in the vain hope that he or she will — just for once — have a smooth ride to work. Yet all know that's not going to happen. So they fret and worry that they will be late.
>
> At every stop along the freeway — which are many — they glance at the clock. The men put on and straighten their strangling neckties. The

women frantically try to put on their make-up, only to end up with the lipstick up one nostril as their car gets nudged from behind.

About an hour later, sometimes two for the truly obsessive, they fight downtown gridlocked traffic to reach their office complex. They wait in line to park their cars in dingy underground lots, paying dearly for the dubious privilege of having their pride and joy get banged, scraped, dented, and gather dust all day.

Then they wait for the elevator. Finally one comes and they shuffle inside, bleary-eyed but eyes down, not acknowledging their fellow sufferers as they squeeze together for a stifling ride to an 80-odd-floor office. Not that the elevator gets there immediately. They must endure more stop-n-go as people scramble to get out at intervening floors, stepping on shoes, elbowing ribs, spilling coffee, and breathing bad breath, as they grunt their way out.

Finally, the commute is almost over. The elevator gets to their destination. With the first sigh of relief since they awoke two or three hours earlier, the commuters trudge off the elevator, unsmilingly mumble a few artificial "Good morning" non-greetings, stash their crumpled coats in an already over-stuffed closet of more crumpled coats, walk to their tiny, noise-invaded, windowless, and stale cubicles, and plop down in uncomfortable chairs to face yet another grueling, unfulfilled day.

After a few minutes' respite to gain their bearings and collect their thoughts, they switch on their computers.

And what do they do all day? They work on the PC and use the phone. That's it!

They sit in their veal-fattening pens (that's what young people call cubicles) and spend their day, without daylight, on the phone or at the computer. At least, that's what they do when they're actually sitting at their desks.

So why the heck didn't they just stay home and do it all from there?

When the dreary day is done, they reverse the entire process. Drag the crumpled coat from the closet, now minus at least one button. Wait for and head back down the stop-n-go elevator. Go back to their newly dented and now-dusty cars. Anxiously seek weather and traffic reports. Wait in line to get out of the parking lot. Nudge back into downtown gridlock. And then finally get back onto the stop-n-go freeway.

Nearing home, another one to two hours later, they stop for gasoline, waiting in line again at busy pumps as fellow commuters fill their tanks for tomorrow's repeat performance. Then they get milk and bread for tomorrow's rushed breakfast.

Finally they arrive home. If they are lucky, they will be in time for dinner. More likely, the rest of the family has eaten and the kids are already in bed again.

Commuters conceive kids, never to see them grow up, except on weekends — "My, hasn't

Johnny changed this week?" Such kids never
see their parents, except on weekends — "Is that
my daddy?"

Other commuters, of course, drop off their
kids, who often are still asleep and unfed, at a
grungy, germ-ridden daycare center. Then they
pick the exhausted kid up again on the way
home.

What are we doing to ourselves, our families, and our way of life?
Like I said, this is an absurd idiocy. Commuters are the "village
idiots" of the global village. A visitor from outer space would find it
bizarre. It's time for it to stop — before it destroys us!

The End of "Going to Work"

To be sure, sensible workers are rethinking where and with whom
they'd genuinely like to live and work.

In terms of "where," just consider this: Does it really matter
whether the critical voice mail, e-mail, or fax you just received was
sent from a client's office, an airport, a traffic jam, or from a home?
Does it matter where you received it? Of course it doesn't.

We are stuck in an antiquated mindset of where, when, how, and
why business takes place. The Internet totally alters the old way of
doing things. And those ways will vanish. In the Internet era, you do
not "go to work." Rather the work comes to you, on your Web appliance, wherever you are.

In the future, to assure a secure and satisfying work–life blend,
most of the next generation of families almost certainly will opt to
work from home in city exurbs and the surrounding countryside.

Telecommuting is most popular in Scandinavia where, as a percentage of the workforce, there are nearly twice as many telecommuters as in the United States and Canada.

Almost 20 percent of U.S. telecommuters live in California. This is not surprising in that five California cities rank in the top ten most-gridlocked cities in the country — San Francisco, Oakland, Los Angeles, San Bernardino, and San Diego. Californians spend about 300,000 hours daily just sitting in traffic — one third of it by Bay Area commuters alone — none of it necessary.

Still, about 54 million Americans and Canadians now work at or from home, of which 36 million telecommute. This compares with a combined total of only 3.7 million telecommuters in 1990. About 34 percent of full-time workers also have somewhat flexible schedules, and the number of remote and mobile workers is soaring. By 2004, more than half the 110-million-strong workforce will be categorized as remote and mobile: telecommuters, road warriors, or bring-work-home types.

Benefits of Telecommuting

Commuting separates neighbors and families — often destroying them. When the farmer went off to work in the textile factory, that was the beginning of the breakdown of the family. Until cars came along, people still knew their neighbors through school, work, and worship. Driving to central workplaces created "bedroom" communities and erased neighborhood links. Today, neighbors often don't even know each other's names. Many career families move into communities fully expecting to be transferred again within two or three years. They don't build relationships, put down roots, or take part in local politics.

The reversal of work back into homes will have exactly the opposite effect. The home-based economic family unit will enhance, restore, and revitalize both family and community stability. About two million North American couples now work together full time from home. And they say it fortifies their marriage.

Our digital homes will be little different from weavers' cottages: spinning wheels, bobbins, and weaving machines are replaced by hard drives, CDs, and PCs. The PC is a "golden loom" weaving data into a rich fabric of wealth that will drive the home-based economy. In addition to wealth creation, telecommuting also

- boosts productivity, with documented gains of up to 70 percent for the same number of hours worked;
- reduces the need for office space and parking spots;
- reduces absenteeism substantially;
- eliminates commuting time and related costs;
- reduces clothing budgets and meal costs;
- provides flexible time scheduling around family time;
- achieves a better blending of work–life activities;
- simplifies childcare and eldercare responsibilities.

Childcare and Eldercare Demands

Regarding the last item on the list, just consider these facts:

- 55 percent of one- to five-year-old North American kids are in some form of daycare while their parents work.
- 25 percent of infants under the age of one year are in a similar situation.

- 30 percent of North American employees are caring for an aging family member.
- 20 percent of employees care both for one or more children *and* one or more aging relatives.

All these percentages are growing, even though fees are going through the roof. And we wonder why families are stressed out?

If your work so severely clashes with your life, then, in my opinion, you really have nowhere to go but out the door. Make the switch and live a real family life in a real neighborhood. I commuted for all 22 years of my banking career. During that entire period, I wasted about 7,000 hours of my life commuting, not including the time needed to dress for the workplace. I also brought home another 7,000 hours of work. In combination, that helped destroy my first marriage.

Since then, I have telecommuted for 21 years as a consultant, author, and public speaker. Sure, some of that involves air travel and time away from home. But I now enjoy a home-based family life and a happy second marriage. Never again would I commute.

That story is not unique. Today, the average big-city worker wastes about 90 minutes on the daily two-way commute. That's 7.5 hours a week or 375 hours over 50 weeks. If they didn't commute, the average downtown worker could instead work four-day weeks at home — or have an extra 10 weeks of annual vacation!

Yet, being more productive working at home, they'd actually get more work done. They also would have more than enough time and money to take proper care of their kids and aging relatives. After all, people working at or from home don't just save oodles of time and lots of money on travel, clothing, and food. They earn more: about

45 percent of telecommuters earn $75,000+ versus only 22 percent of the total workforce.

Also consider the socio-economic and environmental benefits to taxpayers. The U.S. Environmental Protection Agency (EPA) says that if just another 10 percent of workers were to telecommute on only one day a week, it would eliminate 25 million miles of driving frustration, avoid 13,000 tons of air pollutants, and conserve 1.2 million gallons of fuel — all in just one day. Multiply those numbers by five if that 10 percent of workers telecommute every day; double that again if another 10 percent join them.

The beneficial impact on our way of life would be astonishing. Moreover, it costs taxpayers about $1 million per mile to build and maintain freeways. Yet companies need spend only $5,000 per employee to set up and maintain an e-work program.

Tasks Suitable to Telecommuting

Nor can you or your boss argue that your job is not suited to telecommuting. Almost any info-based task is suitable. The first known telecommuter was a Boston bank president. Back in 1877, the year after the telephone's invention, he had a direct phone line strung from his downtown Boston office to his home in suburban Somerville so he could work at home. Telecommuting is most common in banking, insurance, business services, construction, transport, and communications companies. But just about every North American industry has telecommuters.

Obviously, if you are a baker or a dentist, most of your work cannot be done over the phone or the Web, at least not yet. But there is astonishing ignorance about what can and cannot be done online.

Consider just these three examples:

- A senior VP of a U.S. phone company telecommutes full-time from home — in Canada. She oversees 200+ locations worldwide via e-mail and video-conference.

- A visiting nurse in Illinois saves at least 25 hours a week formerly spent driving around greater Chicago by monitoring her patients electronically from home.

- A Florida college professor develops curriculum, teaches accredited online programs globally, and arranges internships for local business employees, from home.

In the face of these trends, most employees are brainwashed to pursue the daily grind and climb the corporate ladder — only to find that the ladder is leaning against the wrong wall. And, as satirical comedienne Lily Tomlin once cracked, "The trouble with the rat race is that even if you win, you're still a rat."

Clearly it's time to quit the rat race. Sure, at first you'll miss kibitzing with colleagues. But that won't last because you'll be with your family instead. It's time to get over the anticipated but mythical "water-cooler withdrawal" and telecommute. And reluctant employers need to join this e-working trend or they'll lose their best people.

One problem is that older Baby Boomers were taught to manage in an industrial economy where the way to perform and get ahead was to "be there." They can't manage other people unless they can see them sitting at a desk, even though, as noted, those desks are mostly empty. Older managers don't trust people, nor do they trust their own ability to manage remote workers.

Those attitudes are changing. Gen-X rejects all that. They grew up with laptops and want to have a mobile lifestyle. They don't want or need to manage people who sit at desks. They know that a virtual team is far superior to workers sitting at desks in a sky-high factory. They manage projects and customer relationships, not workers and paper. They trust people to telecommute.

Telecommuting: Is it Right for You?

Maybe you feel you are just not suited to telecommuting. If you think you need the discipline of a 9-to-5 schedule that forces you to waste seven to ten hours a week commuting and takes you away from your family, then there is no helping you. But I don't believe you have truly thought about it. Nobody gets fulfilled in a cubicle. And, as we've seen, almost anyone can telecommute. Telecommuting will give you lots more time for you and your family, plus time to start your own business on the side.

The idea of going to work is an obsolete factory-era invention. Until then, there was no such thing as a "job" or "wages" or "employees." People went to work for 40+ years at the same firm and hoped to live long enough to retire and get a gold watch. Over the years, the vast majority were not a happy lot. Many said they "loved" their work but fewer than five percent ever really did. Some may have *liked* their job, but they didn't *love* it.

It's the same today with most office workers. They'd rather be doing something else, somewhere else, and for themselves rather than somebody else. And more of them are getting out of the rat race to do just that.

Do you really want to spend up to 100,000 hours of your life, working for someone else — where asking for time off is like asking permission to go to the bathroom — just to end up with a gold watch and, if you're really lucky, maybe a "cool" part-time job as a Wal-Mart greeter?

So try to find a way to quit the "job" world all together and start your own full-time business — something which 16 million North Americans have already done.

Whichever option you select, working at or from home will be a major element of a Web Lifestyle. All truly futuristic families will do it. Are you going to join them?

2

SHOP ONLINE
Have it Delivered!

Every seven seconds, somebody new buys something online for the first time. Then they do it again and again. And it's easy to see why. After all, as I asked in *Future Consumer.Com*, which would *you* rather do?

- Drag the kids to the store, shove a full shopping cart with a wobbly wheel, weaving up and down crowded aisles, wait in line at the checkout (prompting a toddler meltdown), then hump all the stuff home — some three hours later;

Or would you rather:

- Drag the stuff into an online shopping cart with your mouse, faster than writing up a shopping list, then kick back with the kids until it arrives on your doorstep — at the time you select.

A no-brainer, right? That's why the Web is changing how people buy, how often, when, what, why, and from where. Online retail sales grew 21 percent last year.

By 2010, most of us will do much of our shopping online and, as forecast in *Future Consumer.Com*, the Web will account for up to 30 percent of retail sales by then.

Indeed, those who become "prosumers" will buy most things from their very own online store!

The Prosumer Web

There once were few stores of any description. Our ancestors grew their own crops, raised their own hens, cured their own bacon, milked their own cows, baked their own bread and cookies, made their own jam and preserves, even tailored, sewed, and knit their own clothing. They were prosumers — they consumed their own produce.

The factory economy changed all that and brought Main Street stores and then shopping malls. The Web is changing it all again, and 9/11 reinforced the change, driving about 11 percent of shoppers to do *all* of their holiday shopping online from home rather than risk going out to malls.

Despite the 2000 dot-com shakeout and 2001 slowdown, the 2001 year-end holiday shopping seasons saw people flocking online. Nearly 32 million people — or 10 percent of the U.S. and Canadian population — shopped online, spending about $400 each for a total of $12.8 billion. Some eight million of these shoppers had never before bought anything online. All told, about 70 million North Americans now have bought a product online.

As well, 80 percent of holiday shoppers say they saved one to eight hours by shopping online, averaging at least four hours each. While habits are not easy to change, people are slowly changing their shopping routine. And as more families come to appreciate the time and convenience — plus the safety — of e-shopping, online sales can only continue to grow.

Following the surge in online shopping that closed out 2001, and then again in 2002, the debate over whether e-shopping will materialize is over. During the next few years, e-shopping will go mainstream.

By comparison, brick-and-mortar shopping is a pain: crowded parking lots and store aisles, freezing-cold or steamy-hot weather, tired feet and long check-out lines, "out of stock" products and disinterested, discourteous, clueless store clerks — not to mention the drain on your time.

The Web takes shopping out of the shops. In turn, of course, that takes the shops out of shopping and brings them right into your home. Your PC becomes your shop — a virtual showroom for comparison-shopping and convenient buying. And it is stocked with everything from vintage wine to brand new cars.

Products Most Suitable for e-Purchase

You can search for and buy goods from a host of worldwide merchants through your PC at any time of day or night. Web stores never close.

Beyond what we know about what's already selling online, basic common sense tells us what kinds of products are a "no-brainer" to buy online. Some items obviously are easier to buy online than others, depending on three factors:

1. **How complex is the product or service to research, understand, and purchase?** The Web is perfect for at least researching, if not buying, almost any product or service.

2. **How easy/inexpensive is the product to get delivered to your home, or to return if you don't want it?** Products other than purely digitized ones — such as

software, music, books, or videos — still must be physically delivered to your home. But even if you needed
a pound of nails, on which the shipping costs would be
prohibitive, you could still order online and then pick
them up at the store, maybe at a drive-through. And,
as with mail-order catalogs, you can always return any
product you don't want.

3. **Do you really need to see, touch, try on, or test it?**
Many argue that you need to see, touch, feel, and try
every product before you buy it. That can be true for
fresh grocery items, some clothing, furniture and appliances, and perhaps major purchases such as cars and
homes. But not everybody needs to squeeze tomatoes,
try on new slacks, lie down on a new bed, test drive a
car, or walk through a home before buying it. Today,
all these products are already being bought online,
sight unseen.

So online shopping is all about time, convenience, and cost.

Four Product Types

Products thus can be viewed as being of four types, as follows.

• *Convenience Items*

Simple, lightweight convenience items are the easiest
to buy online and to have delivered to your home. In
addition, on the Web anything that can be digitized
will be digitized. And digitized items can be easily
delivered by downloading them. The Web thus simplifies and speeds up the purchase of any low-research

items. Convenience items are among the hottest online sellers. They include books, music, videos, tickets, toys, flowers, newspapers, greetings cards, collectibles, and car and home insurance. About 12 percent of book sales now occur online.

• *Replenishment Items*

The next easiest products you can buy online are replenishment items, such as non-perishable food and cleaning products. You simply replace the product as your on-hand supply runs out. These somewhat bulkier items might incur heavier shipping costs. But they require no research on your part after your first purchase. Happy with the product, you buy it again and again, almost without thinking about it. Just think about how many of the items in your supermarket shopping cart are the very same items you buy over and over again, week in, week out. Why not just have those replenishment items delivered? Examples are detergent, cleaning items, pet food, vitamins, cosmetics, underwear, socks, shoes, home-office supplies, tools, hardware, and garden supplies.

• *Researched Items*

Slightly more difficult to buy online are items such as life insurance, mortgage loans, travel packages, or computer software. They are relatively easy to get delivered, either digitally online or by courier.

However, they tend to be complex items that can require some consideration and perhaps expert advice. For example, life insurance is less straightforward than car insurance, and consumer electronics come in a host of choices that you need to compare. Still, the Web is remarkably effective in helping you with research on these items, and many of them are bought online. For example, 46 percent of common stocks are bought and sold online.

• *Subjective Items*

The most difficult items to buy online and have delivered to your home are bulky and heavy products that also require much research — increasingly now done online — and tend to be bought at brick-and-mortar stores. However, the Web again is a big help, even in the purchase of research-intensive, subjective products such as automobiles and homes. The Web greatly simplifies and speeds up the time-consuming pre-purchase process. As well, all these items are being bought online — yes, sight unseen — some of them quite strongly. Examples are computers, furniture and appliances, sports equipment, automobiles, home and building supplies, and even homes. Last year, the Internet accounted for 18 percent of computer hardware and software sales.

Clearly, then, every product type is already being bought online. So the Web obviously can handle even complex purchases.

Much of this success is because the Web also lets you interact with the product. For example, Amazon lets you peek inside books and to submit personal preferences of book genres or authors to get automatic notification of new books or suggested titles of interest.

The Web also helps you buy products that are more personalized or customized to your tastes and needs. Dell lets you custom-build your PC online and the car companies are planning to let you do the same when you buy a WebMobile.

There really is no excuse not to shop online. Soon, most of us will be shopping this way, not just for books and PCs but for health-care products, groceries, and almost all our everyday needs.

Doorstep Delivery

As noted, most of the items we buy are convenience or replenishment items that we buy over and over again, week in, week out. We write out the same shopping list every week and trudge off to spend a couple of hours in a supermarket, gathering up hefty items, almost walking down the aisles blindfolded and as we pick them off the same spot on the shelves as last week.

Supermarkets, of course, are a relatively modern, 1950s-era invention. So are packaged goods. Most products once came from a local general store, grocery store, or butcher, and were weighed out on an item-by-item, order-by-order basis by the shopkeeper. Many of these family-run businesses also delivered the orders to their customers' homes.

I recall how my mother did the family shopping in rural post-War England. She had two pocket-sized Order Books. Every week, she wrote out the order on a fresh page in one of the books: 1-lb sugar, 1-

lb butter, 2-lb flour, and so on. The grocer weighed out the products into plain brown bags and packed them into a wooden crate for delivery to the house. My mother paid him for the amount tallied in the Order Book and handed him the second Order Book that listed next week's items. And so it went: take delivery of one week's order and send back the Order Book for next week.

But the lists never varied much from one week to the next. She ordered much the same items as before. In fact, 90 percent of the items on each page in both books were the same as for every other week. I once asked her why she just didn't send the same list back again, rather than copying it out each time. She said that would be handy, but the itemized lists with the grocer's prices entered alongside each product helped her to remember what to buy and to manage her tight shopping budget. She could vary the items and their quantities to stay in budget — there was no credit in those days; it was cash on delivery.

The shopping Webolution returns us to those days. It is now possible to order not just replenishment items, but any type of product online by simply checking off boxes on automatic re-order forms and then have it all delivered. It's far quicker than writing up a brand new list for your needless trip to the supermarket and you can better manage your weekly household budget.

So far, the best example of such a service is Quixtar's "Ditto Delivery" program. You submit a standing order for replenishment items but can still vary it to suit your changing needs or grocery budget.

Yet the supermarkets fail to grasp the customer demand for this service. According to survey data from Food Marketing Institute, only 14 percent of U.S. supermarkets think home delivery is important and only 20 percent are the least bit concerned about online competition. Only one in four supermarkets offers any kind of home shopping or home delivery program.

By contrast, the U.K.-based Tesco chain is a roaring online success, grabbing 80 percent of Britain's online grocery market and becoming the world's largest online grocer. Moreover, its online profit margins are more than double those of its brick-and-mortar business. Tesco is now joining forces with Safeway in the U.S. and Canada to bring online grocery shopping to North America and it is only a matter of time before millions of us will be shopping that way.

Why not join them and take another step toward living the future and a Web Lifestyle?

3
BANK ONLINE
e-Manage Your Money

Digits are replacing currency. And thanks to WebPhones and PCs, managing your money will never be the same.

Instead of waiting in line at bank tellers and machines, millions of us now bank online. Even that will change. Very soon, your WebPhone will replace everything you now carry in your wallet or purse. Everything ... well, except lipstick!

No more coins, bills, checks, wads of credit cards, driving license, social security and health cards, passport, family photos, appointment book, or business cards to clutter your life.

Just a handy-dandy, wireless, digital, multimedia appliance that safeguards all your personal papers, the WebPhone will even keep track of your financial affairs and automatically file your tax returns.

You'll use it to shop and pay for everything, transferring money from your WebPhone to someone else's as simply as handing spending money to your kids. Simply point your WebPhone at a vending machine and a can of pop will tumble out.

As mobile as your watch, as personal as your purse, but safer than either, your fingerprint-secure WebPhone will be worthless to a thief and, should it get lost, you'll have a backup copy at home.

Future Money

Whatever is the most current always becomes society's currency. Today, what is most current is the flow of digital information. Now, money is purely digital — information on the move. Electronic blips, representing trillions of dollars, flow daily through electronic networks as easily as a coin drops into a parking meter.

Throughout history, money has always changed with the underlying technology of the day. Seashells, pebbles, and grains of rice were among the earliest forms of money. The metal age brought coins around 700 BC and paper money appeared in the late 1600s. IOUs, bank drafts, and check forms soon followed. The petroleum age brought plastic: credit cards and then debit cards.

Online, the credit card itself — or rather its account number (you don't need the plastic) — essentially has become *the* digital currency medium. Credit cards are used in 98 percent of all online payment transactions — in contrast to some 24 percent of offline consumer spending. Yet some people are afraid to use credit cards online. Go figure!

As well, software now gives you a "digital wallet" that lets you simply enter your credit card info once and store it securely in a wallet icon on your PC. This eliminates the tedious need to repeatedly enter your name, address, and credit card details when filling out online order forms. It thus makes the plastic card itself irrelevant.

Some credit cards are becoming smartcards. Smartcards are "smart" because of a computer chip embedded in the plastic. Again, you only need the plastic so you don't lose the chip. The chip holds much more information than does the black magnetic stripe on the back of standard cards. Smartcards are very popular in Europe and will increasingly be used worldwide.

The Target discount store chain, with nearly a thousand stores and more than 36 million customer accounts, is the first major U.S. retailer to issue a smartcard. The co-branded Visa card replaces Target's existing "Guest" card. Target also supplies a free card-reading device for home PCs so that consumers can shop online and even download electronic coupons.

Consumers in Japan can now pay for taxi rides, car washes, newspapers, and other routine purchases through WebPhones that contain a smartcard-like chip. In Europe, you can download cash from your bank account, just as if you were at an automated teller machine (ATM), through the airwaves and into a Nokia phone for later use. In Finland, point a Nokia WebPhone at a vending machine and a can of Coke tumbles out; the price is added to your phone bill.

You thought I was kidding, didn't you?

Information About Money

Against this background, your financial service provider is not so much in the money business but the business of information *about* money. The obvious example is the banking machine. When you use a banking machine you don't visit a machine but a digital network where you conduct an electronic transaction in real time. Hence, your bank is a digital information network.

Eventually, banking machines will be replaced by WebPhones and online banking. The banking machine has been teaching us how to handle our financial affairs electronically. I've used bank machines since 1972 and now bank online. My daughters naturally think the ATM or the PC *is* the bank. Having grown up with this technology, it is perfectly normal for them to think of it as the natural way of doing things. So it will be with the Web for all financial services, not just deposits, withdrawals, and bill payments.

Again, skeptics abound, especially in the moribund banking, stock brokerage, and insurance industries. In 1998, the vice-chair of Merrill Lynch actually denounced the Internet as a "serious threat to Americans' financial lives." Within weeks, the lumbering broker woke up to reality and did an about-face, posting all its stock research, free of charge, on its website.

Mutual funds, stocks and bonds, insurance, credit cards, bill payment, mortgages, and installment credit are all currently being sold and serviced by mail, telephone, kiosk, PC, and — very soon — pocket-sized WebPhones.

That will put your banker in your pocket!

Digital Money Dashboard

In the near future, any "with it" financial service firm will digitally deliver to you a real-time, personalized "money dashboard" that constantly updates your entire financial situation in a single window on your PC screen, as you can do at Yodlee or CashEdge.

Intuit's Quicken service also lets you handle virtually all your financial information online, including credit card, bank, and brokerage accounts. You can make your tax payments, buy insurance, prepare for college education, or plan your retirement.

Such services will alert you to bills requiring payment, dividends coming due, and so on, along with a complete balance sheet and earnings statement with projected future cash flows.

They will alert you to investment opportunities such as the chance to buy stocks on technical dips in price. You also will be offered pre-approved mortgage refinancing and other loans, based on the updated strength of your net financial position and projected future prospects.

Quicken is rolling out stock portfolio and tax advisory tools that offer "vignettes" or scenarios of your financial potential based on your current situation and particular financial goals.

So who needs a brick-and-mortar bank? By the end of 2005, the number of U.S. and Canadian households banking online is expected to triple, from 18 million today to about 54 million.

As mentioned earlier, 46 percent of all stock trades are already done online. By contrast, only two percent of insurance policies are bought online. But at InsureMarket.com you can even pay for policies online by credit card.

Perhaps the most natural insurance to gravitate online will be commodity-type policies such as home and car insurance. For example, Progressive lets you pay for car insurance electronically, with premiums based on mileage that is monitored electronically. Normally, auto insurance premiums are based on risk factors such as your age and driving record, your marital status, and the age and model of the vehicle. The company sensibly believes these factors are less important than how much you use the car and when and where you drive it. The company thus monitors the miles you drive and the routes you take via a tracking box affixed to the car, capturing that data via cellphone and satellite. As a result, insurance premiums have dropped by an average of 25 percent.

More complicated policies such as health insurance also might be a natural for the Web. Most health insurance is carried privately in the U.S. and research shows that the vast majority of online

Americans who have health insurance would prefer to manage their coverage on the Web. This preference reflects a deep frustration with healthcare red tape and bureaucracy.

In response, American International Group (AIG), which processes about 500,000 claims by phone, fax and mail, has put self-serve claim features online. You enter your own data and can view your claim history. This saves time and money, averts errors, and reduces your frustration by giving you a claim number instantly.

Write Your Own Mortgage

These days, the quickest and easiest way to finance a home is to get a mortgage from any of 100+ mortgage-related websites. These sites help you decide whether you should rent or buy, just how much home you can really afford, and how tax breaks will play out. Most sites let you figure out a 15- to 30-year loan, at a variety of interest rates and taking into account any fees.

The top e-lender, E-Loan, saves you as much as 80 percent on loan fees. It offers all types of loans, from fixed and adjustable rate mortgages to auto loans and credit cards. It even provides relocation services if you move house more than one hundred miles. Quicken Mortgage also provides online pre-approvals and locked-in interest rates. And with rates at 60-year lows, there has never been a better time to buy a home — the very best investment that you will ever make.

On this point, I must disagree with Robert Kiyosaki, author of the best-selling *Rich Dad, Poor Dad* books, which do otherwise contain valuable insights. But he argues that a home is a liability, not an asset. This is an incredible view from somebody peddling financial advice. Trust me, the home you own is an asset.

History shows that property always increases in value over time. Studies also show that the average return on investment of the average home, over time, is at least seven percent per annum — often more, depending on how much you paid, how you financed it, and the growth in your housing market. I will always own a home that I can afford over any other item. It's the best asset — and investment — you can have.

Buy at least one! You can do it all online, just as our family did with our vacation home. And, yes, it's fully wired for the Web Lifestyle.

4
SCHOOL @ HOME
e-Learn a Living!

The web takes schooling out of the schools. More than two million North American kids already do their learning at home.

While that's just four percent of the K–12 population, the number is growing 12 percent a year and will top five million by 2010 or sooner — especially as more parents will telecommute.

The major turning point for home schooling was the Columbine school shooting rampage. Other worries are endemic drug use, overcrowded classrooms, and stagnating educational quality.

Seriously questioning the curriculum's suitability in a fast-changing world, parents rightly fret about their kids' future career success.

Together, these worries are leading more and more families to opt for either private schools or home schooling — or a blend of the two.

The terrorism threat and the Internet opportunity will draw more and more families and adult learners to these options, with both private and home schooling growing in strength throughout the next decade.

Mass classroom education will not be able to compete with individualized learning at home. By 2010, many public school, college, and university campuses could stand empty.

Taking Schooling Out of the Schools

As the ranks of U.S. and Canadian home-schooling families have grown, they've also changed dramatically. At one time, home schooling was a fringe movement where parents cited religious beliefs as the main reason for teaching their kids themselves.

But a 2001 study by the U.S. Department of Education shows that home schooling is going mainstream. For example, home-schooling parents have the same average income as those in the public system. These parents select home schooling believing it gives their kids a better education. Religion is not the issue.

Another motivator, though, is school violence, which has become intolerable to a growing number of parents and kids. After the Columbine and other school shootings and stabbings, millions of parents wonder, "Is my kid's school next?"

Even without such terror, the National Education Association estimates that close to 200,000 kids skip school each day because of peer intimidation. A study by the National Institute of Health finds that almost a third of sixth to tenth graders — six million kids across the U.S.A. — have experienced some kind of bullying.

Now, home schooling is far from an easy matter. You're not simply dropping off your kids at school every morning for somebody else to educate. So it may not be for everyone. But parents who teach their children at home find they have closer relationships with them and that the kids are more confident and independent.

In some American states, many charter schools ally themselves with home schooling parents, offering structure and support such as books and a curriculum to follow at home. Some charter schools also arrange "park days," museum visits, and other field trips for home school children to come together and socialize in a learning environment.

Other families fed up with public schools elect to send their kids to private schools, especially those with Montessori programs. These have very low teacher-pupil ratios, often as low as seven or eight kids to one teacher.

While this is not home schooling, where the ratio is more like two or three kids to one parent, private school parents also spend a lot of time helping their kids with homework and special assignments. They turn their home into a learning environment focused on the kids. In this way, they treat the private school as if they are hiring a private tutor where the kids go to class to get professional guidance and to learn how to socialize with others.

Other parents are flocking online for help, going to sites such as InternetHomeSchool.com which provides online curricula for Grades 1–12. It also has daily check-ins and weekly work samples to keep home scholars focused, plus self-paced lessons for Grades 1–8 based on learning activities and downloadable worksheets.

Our family uses a mixture of these options. Our daughters go to a private Montessori school that has small classes. At home, they use educational toys, books, puzzles, crafts, videos, and selective TV programs. They use the PC to interact with educational CDs and suitable websites. They also go to educational community activities and creative-learning programs of various kinds.

No matter which option you select, as a home school parent you can rest easy about your kids' college future. For starters, home school children do better on their SAT scores: 1093 average versus 1020 for public school kids. And universities are relaxing their admission requirements to attract these better-educated teens. As well, many college admission directors say the Internet has more than leveled the field between home-school and high-school kids. After all, the vast majority of today's Web-savvy kids learned to use a computer at home, not at school.

George Washington Didn't Go to School

Home schooling is not new. The farmhouse kitchen once was the classroom and mother was the teacher. While some grammar schools and universities were founded in the Middle Ages, the vast majority of children still learned at home from their parents and — for the well-to-do — from a hired tutor or governess.

Early American presidents such as George Washington, James Madison, and John Quincy Adams never went to school. Not until after the Civil War did "little red schoolhouse" learning become the North American norm.

Distance education began as long ago as the 1700s in Europe, where students mailed written exercises to their professors who, in turn, graded and sent the exercises back by mail. In 1840, Sir Isaac Pitman taught secretarial skills by having students translate the Bible into shorthand, mailing their squiggles back to him for grading.

Even as late as 1924, there still were four times as many people taking correspondence courses with private firms as were attending colleges, universities, and professional schools.

Industrial-era factory-like schooling then brought mass public education. John and Jane went off to school. The problem with factory schools is that they force everyone to learn at the same pace, virtually killing most learning before it even happens. By contrast to mass education, the computer offers a chance to move everyone to a model of individualized learning.

As well, of course, today's complex world of constant change makes knowledge obsolete very quickly. So the curriculum is often inappropriate, especially now. As one student reflected after 9/11, "We've been taught more about how to deconstruct and dissect rather than to construct or decide." Education anyway can no longer be acquired from out-of-date textbooks during youth and then be expected to serve for an entire lifetime. Rather, learning must be a continuous process, culled from constantly updated content.

Fortunately, the Web offers a new form of interactive learning that allows almost anyone to learn virtually anything, anywhere, at any time. The future requires just-in-time learning where students can "dial a tutor" — a life mentor — anywhere in cyberspace. Mass education can never compete with that, and it inevitably will be replaced by individualized, lifelong e-learning via the Web.

e-Learning is Fun

The word "school" comes from "skol," meaning "fun." And most learning and creativity, especially at early ages, happens at home and occurs through play. Creative parents encourage forms of play that involve high learning potential. With a little encouragement they turn ordinary playtime into learning that sparks the child's imagination and builds an appetite for yet more learning. Once their child can operate a mouse, they expose the child to creative software and suitable websites.

Futuristic parents see the PC and the Web as valuable tools to build family cohesion by finding common interests or learning projects to do together online. They build what Seymour Papert in *The Connected Family* calls a "family learning culture."

At the age of two, for example, our daughter Melissa learned to maneuver a computer mouse as handily as a crayon in two minutes. At age three, she could boot up the laptop, insert a CD, load a program or go online, and simply have fun while learning. In turn, at age four, Melissa is now showing her two-year-old sister Ashley how to do the same.

It's almost easier for a Web-Gen kid to install software and surf the Web than to open a pencil box and scribble down notes copied from a screeching-chalk-on-faded-gray slate blackboard. That's so Stone Age! Modern teachers use colored markers on whiteboards that also serve as virtual computer screens. Such teachers and their students surf the Web — and the curriculum — together.

Today's "screenage" kids live in homes with online PCs and use them eagerly. Indeed, 92 percent of them used a PC before their eighth birthday and soon became experts. Of the time they spend online, two-thirds of it comes from TV watching, one-third from playing video games. That in itself is a good trend. Teens say website surfing is as easy as TV channel surfing and "a more natural thing to do." They say the Web is "more fun" than TV and, more important, that it is "the most fun" way to learn!

Not surprisingly, 93 percent of parents say a PC is the most beneficial product they can buy for their children. A similar percentage of PC owners cite their children's education as the main reason for buying — ahead of their own work-at-home and financial application needs. Parents who said, *"Turn off the TV and do your homework!"* now say, *"Turn on your PC and do your homework!"*

In many homes, the PC long ago displaced encyclopedias, dictionaries, and textbooks as the best learning resource. Two-thirds of children with a PC at home use it to do homework and 85 percent of them complete assignments with information found online.

The Web is fantastic for letting people go out and explore things on their own. It can turn every home into a living classroom. With PCs, homework is not hard work; it's fun. In PC households, the average amount of time spent on homework increases by more than two hours a week. And the majority of students who use the Web for online research feel more confident about their assignments. Not surprisingly, various surveys find that students with PCs also get better grades.

Learning is most fun — and more effective — when the content is most captivating and engaging. Multimedia PCs captivate the imagination: they show live events, animatedly illustrate concepts, and provide meaning and emotion through words and music — all in engagingly interactive ways that challenge, entice, and excite eager young minds.

For example, much to the chagrin of English literature teachers, you can even study Shakespeare much better by computer. Yes, *much* better! Teachers forget that Shakespeare wrote his plays to be performed live on stage, not to be read from books. In fact, most people in Shakespeare's day couldn't read.

Students thus can read an e-text of *Richard III* alongside a windowed movie version starring Sir Laurence Olivier, the best Shakespearian actor of all time. They can zoom in for close-ups, do camera pans, and search the text for words and character names, pop up a dictionary explaining obscure words, or click on tutorials about the plot and characters — all at their own speed, on their own time, based on their own needs. No lit teacher can ever do that.

My kingdom for a PC?

Cheap Chips versus Costly Bricks

Whether there ever will be a PC on every classroom desk is not worth considering. The educational Webolution is already taking place in the home. The home PC is changing the way we write, compute, communicate, and learn. It has whetted the appetite for individual educational experiences that mass education can never achieve. To put PCs in schools and connect them to the Internet is to perpetuate a failed system. We need to do exactly the opposite.

We need to take the learning to the learner, at home. So rather than putting schools online, we should use the Web to replace schools with "Webucation." Web-based training cuts education budgets at least in half. Money is being spent in all the wrong places: in brick-and-mortar lecture halls and libraries that sit unused for months on end.

College students anyway take notes on a laptop, their clicking keyboards a constant companion to the lecture. Indeed, websites such as StudentU.com hire university students to take lecture notes, and then put them online within 24 hours for free download.

Inevitably, this will lead to a drop in attendance. Ultimately, the only two people there will be the prof and the note taker!

Long before that happens, of course, the best profs will smarten up and place their own notes online for an e-university that also "got the message" and went virtual.

So we should be creating electronic campuses. One cabinet-sized

200-terabit server could replace thousands of libraries and schools, as well as administrators, and teachers. Web-based training serves up instruction anywhere, year round, around the clock, with vastly reduced admin costs.

Students also avoid commuting or travel costs, "attending" class according to their own schedule. They can choose from courses offered by a wide variety of cyber-schools worldwide, seeking out the planet's best online instructors.

If all education were digitized, the cost of education would drop at least ten-fold. Why don't they just do it?

Parents and taxpayers truly worried about the cost of schooling should force schools to seriously explore the Web as an alternative. And home-schooling parents should lobby for a huge tax credit, in lieu of helping reduce the burden on the nation.

Student Interaction Online

What about classroom interaction? Any who argue that nothing can replace class interaction clearly haven't been online. Today's virtual professors post their assignments online and send graded papers across the Web. They find that online students can learn just as well if not better than those forced to sit in banked lecture halls.

Online students cannot sit passively in the back row twiddling their thumbs. They must think and communicate with a virtual prof who can pose a question at any moment and, within 30 seconds, get responses from every student — and know immediately who has and hasn't replied. This creates an interactive learning experience where everyone is in the virtual front row — and paying attention.

True education is independent of time and place and is individ-

ual; it occurs not on a campus but in a student's mind, through neural interaction. That's exactly the opposite of today's system which is
over-focused on memorizing facts, poured into the cranium with a
funnel. There's no true knowledge absorption, no neural interaction
with the knowledge, and hence no true learning.

Futuristic education focuses on how our senses learn. The brain
is a multi-disciplinary sensorium. The false division of the curriculum
into separate subjects is limiting because any subject taken in depth
at once relates to other subjects. The Web immerses the senses, making it a perfect vehicle for multi-disciplinary synthesis, for sensorial,
interactive, one-to-one learning.

Moreover, e-learning can provide millions of people with opportunities they may otherwise not obtain — all in a highly efficient,
cost-effective and more businesslike manner. In the future, students
will be able to get a degree without ever leaving home, tuning in
wherever they are, and will have a university education at their beck
and call.

As brick-and-mortar schools continue to lose students to private
and online schools, this will force the public systems to adapt to parents' needs. In turn, the idea will continue to catch on, school district by school district, reshaping education as we know it. And
online learning will become a distinguishing mark of the Web
Lifestyle family.

5
SELF-DOCTOR
Heal Thyself @ Home!

The health system is dangerous to your health. A lumbering bureaucracy full of change-resistant doctors, its arteries are so blocked that we're all at risk.

Remember the days when doctors made house calls? Well, the Baby Boom–driven trend toward a healthier lifestyle, together with new tele-medicine gadgetry, sees increasing numbers of people doing their own doctoring at home.

The Internet is rewriting the implicit contract between doctor and patient. Some 60 percent of Americans and Canadians search for health info online. Many show up at the doctor's office for a physical with website printout in hand.

Millions of people now see their doctor only when absolutely necessary. For example, asthma, diabetic, and heart patients can routinely download their vital signs and daily test results to their caregivers.

This self-care trend will spread to more and more patient segments as tele-medicine becomes even easier and cheaper — and safer than visits to germ-ridden doctors' offices and medical centers.

In turn, electronic house calls — by doctors, nurses, and other caregivers — will become an everyday part of a Web Lifestyle.

Hospitals are Dangerous to Your Health!

In North American healthcare generally, only 29 percent of physicians use a computer of any sort to access patient information. Only 37 percent use the Internet for anything, mostly for e-mail. In non-digital hospitals, it is estimated that physicians waste up to 60 percent of their day just hunting for patient data. No wonder, then, that 40 percent of critical data is missing when doctors need it, leading to deadly errors. Indeed, a 1999 report by the Institute of Medicine said that as many as 98,000 people die annually from medical mistakes. That's one person every five minutes!

Like I said, the health system is dangerous to your health.

Due to the shortage of tech-savvy physicians, there is strong resistance to the use of computer and Web-based systems. Doctors indirectly control about 80 percent of healthcare resources and won't spend the money on technology they don't comprehend.

But this will have to change. Newly qualified doctors take information technology for granted and refuse to work without it. Only digitized hospitals will attract them. As well, starting in 2003 in America, the Health Insurance Portability and Accountability Act mandates standards for exchanging and safeguarding patient information, which must be done electronically.

The technology is already here and available. Digital imaging replaces film and lets multiple doctors view the same image instantly. Digitization converges cumbersome paper medical records and charts into a single electronic patient record. Digital prescriptions and test results cut the number of serious medication errors in half.

Failure to adopt these technologies is nothing less than a form of medical malpractice. Class action suit, anyone?

Many patients now find more help in cyberspace than in their own doctors' offices. While less than 10 percent of online users are aware of a website operated by their own doctor, about 75 percent of them say they'd prefer to use one.

As a result, doctors who fail to provide online access will suffer increased patient turnover in their medical practices. As patients become better informed and more assertive about their care, they will insist on better service from healthcare providers.

Faced with this dilemma, the American Medical Association (AMA), which together with other groups represents more than 400,000 doctors, belatedly woke up from its self-imposed tele-medicine anesthesia. In late 1999, AMA launched a new company called Medem, a name derived from the "medical empowerment" concept. Medem has signed up thousands of doctors for a "YourMD" service. Now, no doctor has any excuse not to go online.

YourMD sets up doctors with a customized website, secure e-mail connections with patients and colleagues, patient-education materials, and the newest info related to their medical specialties.

But that's still a meager response to a cholesterol-ridden health-care system. Compare that with WebMD.com which features online chats with experts, message boards, medical updates, and a medical library and drug reference guide. You also can customize the site so that you can keep informed on specific illnesses.

"Web-Informed" Patients

In the future, the Web-informed patient — not the doctor — will drive the healthcare system. Tech-savvy patients resist being treated stereotypically for condition "x" and want customized attention.

Seeking increased control over their health through personalized treatments, patients will routinely go online to download their health info, get e-diagnoses from doctors and other caregivers, review their own charts, and track their own treatment plans.

People increasingly show self-reliance in maintaining their physical and mental well-being. The more knowledgeable people are, they usually make better lifestyle and healthcare decisions, and play a much more active role in their self-care. Anyone with Web access who faces a health crisis can easily find info on procedures, new therapies, and even innovative treatments not yet covered by their health plan.

In our family, my wife does most of the online health searching. Women do 80 percent of the searching for health info because they make most healthcare decisions within a family. More than 60 percent of the health info that users read online is family related, usually for children or aging parents.

In fact, a key factor driving this demand for health info is the aging population. Older adults use about five times as many drug prescriptions per year as healthy midlife adults. Not surprisingly, Web users aged 40+ are at least 50 percent more likely to go online for health info than their younger counterparts.

It's also easy to conduct a widening array of healthcare transactions online: comparing insurance rates, signing up for insurance, submitting health status updates, and buying prescription drugs. Already, healthcare is a larger e-business than books and music. In 2001, North Americans spent $256 billion on wellness, from fitness clubs to vitamins and prescriptions. Total wellness spending will top $1 trillion by 2010, much of it online.

Direct sellers and network marketers such as Quixtar are positioned to become the dominant online distributors of wellness and nutritional products that health-conscious people are using in record numbers as they treat themselves at home and over the Web.

At-Home Tele-Medicine

As noted, treat-yourself medical devices also are proliferating.

Asthma patients, for example, can use a pocket-size airway monitor called AirWatch that records breathing. Hooked to a phone line, it sends data to a computer and, within minutes, a report is sent to the doctor for review. Monthly, the doctor and patient both get a report on how well the asthma is responding to medication.

Similarly, diabetics can monitor their blood-sugar readings online. They prick a finger, squeeze a tiny drop of blood onto a glucose meter, connect that to their PC, and zap the result to their doctor to see if they need to modify medication. Savvy patients can decide for themselves what needs changing. You now can even check your blood sugar on a PDA and chart the results.

Some heart pacemaker patients now transmit data over phone lines to their doctors. But that's just the beginning. Device maker Medtronic is launching a service where heart patients with pacemakers, defibrillators and other implants will transmit their up-to-the-minute cardiac data over the Web to cardiologists. (Defibrillators are used to shock a quivering heart back to a normal rhythm.) Ultimately the data will download automatically without patients doing anything, even while they are asleep.

The information could include heart rate, the status of the electrical lead connecting the device to the heart, and the status of its battery. Caregivers even will be able to reprogram the device by sending directions to the patient's home over the Web. Or they could change the medication and order up a modified prescription.

Even serious wounds can be monitored from a distance. For example, American TeleCare equipment allows a "video visit" evaluation of a patient's condition right in their home. Evaluated visually and verbally, patients are checked out on heart, lung, and bowel sounds, plus blood pressure. Using high resolution video, the clinician can view wounds and dressings, as well as readings on blood glucose and oxygen meters, IV pumps, and so on — all in about three minutes.

A similar, non-video system by HomMed lets patients do much of this themselves, taking just a few keystrokes to download the data, either wirelessly or by phone. These remote devices allow a single nurse to watch over and interact with 500 patients without having to visit each one at their home.

In fact, an online medicine cabinet has been designed that uses face-recognition to identify different household members and their special needs. Sensors on prescription bottles help the cabinet to identify each drug so it can alert patients if they take the wrong bottle — or the right bottle at the wrong time. The cabinet also can monitor vital signs, chart them for the patient, and transmit the data to the doctor's office.

That's not all. The Japanese have invented a health-monitoring toilet that examines stool and urine for unhealthy levels of sugar, blood, fiber, and fat. The toilet also measures your weight, body temperature, and blood pressure. If something is seriously amiss, the toilet sends data to your doctor's office for electronic consultation.

Automated external defibrillators are being deployed in public places (such as malls, airports, and stadiums), often alongside fire extinguishers, for use by co-workers, travelers, and passersby. The device is fool-proof — it won't shock hearts that have a normal rhythm — and infinitely easier to use than trying to perform CPR on a patient. The device uses simple visual and audible cues to guide the rescuer through the crucial minutes, providing attention much faster than waiting for paramedics to arrive.

Devices such as digital medicine cabinets, defibrillators, and health-monitoring toilets are forerunners to comprehensive clinic stations that will become commonplace in public places and in our homes. And all these and more Web-based applications mean that many fewer of us will have to sit in germ-ridden waiting rooms, exposed to contagious illnesses, coughs, and sneezes.

And that has to be a blessing!

e-Charts and e-Medic Alerts

Some healthcare providers are starting to use Internet-linked PC tablets to check patients' lab test results, input vital signs, order medications, and perform other quick transactions. Such electronic pen tablets are replacing charts at the patient's bedside.

In the future, every patient will carry a smartcard, a key-ring tag, or a bracelet charm that stores all their medical info. This computer-readable "e-medic alert" will detail chronic diseases, immunizations, hospitalizations, operations, treatment files, x-rays, lab results, blood donor info, medications, allergies, insurance info — the list goes on. By 2005 or so, your entire medical history, including your genome sequence, could be stored on your e-medic alert and/or your WebPhone. Paramedics, on picking up a patient, will wirelessly read the gadget into a diagnostic machine that both displays the patient's history and downloads it to doctors waiting in the hospital emergency department.

Injuries will be x-rayed for instant viewing both in the ambulance and back at the hospital. The paramedics will video-chat with doctors on call who can see and talk with the patient and the paramedic to administer the most appropriate *en route* care.

Smartcards are also reducing the enormous admin costs that soak up nearly 30 percent of total annual healthcare budgets in North America. Insurance companies, for example, process nearly five billion claims a year, most of them manually. Paperless systems are starting to reduce this enormous burden.

RealMed is giving smartcards to patients and installing software at doctors' offices for a digital network that links patient, practitioner, and insurer. The patient presents the smartcard to the doctor, the system verifies insurance eligibility, and data are automatically sent to the payment center for authorization.

Apart from big cost savings, the system slashes the reimbursement time from a frustrating 42 days to just four minutes.

Health Plans Go Online

Another factor driving online healthcare demand is the shift to managed health plans in the United States and the related transfer of greater responsibility for healthcare to patients themselves.

Many commercial and Blue Cross/Blue Shield health plans provide Web-based services to members. Health plan websites offer benefit plan summaries and eligibility details, claims status updates, glossaries of medical terms, and answers to frequently asked questions. As well, you can submit inquiries via e-mail, download printable claim forms, and order replacement ID cards.

WebMD.com, again, links doctors and insurers so they can process workers' compensation and automobile injury claims online. The company is the largest online processor of medical claims — about two billion annually. It also has an alliance with AOL to provide health content via co-branded websites where patients can communicate with doctors and health plan providers. Doctors can call up patient records and insurance info, and patients can schedule appointments, see lab results, and renew prescriptions online.

e-Pharmacies Eliminate Illegible Rx Slips

Chicken-scratch drug prescriptions — more than three billion annually in North America — are also being digitized. For example, the Allscript e-prescription pad lets doctors submit a patient's drug order through a pocket device, either to a pharmacy or a courier.

Walgreen.com, the website of America's largest drugstore chain, provides patients with same-day delivery or pick-up at a local store. Prescription insurance programs are accepted online and you can access your prescription history. The site also provides details on potential drug interactions, health and wellness info from the Mayo Clinic, and prescription-order status checks.

You get e-mail reminders for new and refill prescriptions and, if you wish, reminders of doctor's appointments. You can also e-mail questions to the "Ask Your Pharmacist" section.

Online pharmacies operate in a very similar fashion to their mail-service counterparts. They carry huge selections of everything from Aspirin to Zantac, and offer three big advantages: the privacy of ordering at home, time-saving (in the form of no waiting at prescription counters), plus the convenience of home delivery.

Taken together, these trends are the prescription for a major healthcare Webolution. By 2010, tele-medicine will be a routine part of health maintenance for the Web Lifestyle family.

6
DIGITIZE YOUR FUN
Download It!

Families that surf together — and laugh together — will stay togeth-er. By 2010, all but a few families will be online and much enter-tainment will occur at home — just as it did pre-radio and pre-TV.

With the Web, anything that can be digitized will be digitized and downloaded. Already, more than 60 million North American adults download wholesome fun in four big categories — music, games, movies, and sports — onto PCs or into fast-converging PC-TV large-screen "home theaters."

Yes, people will still attend live events and play sports. But the reality of sitting way back in a large crowd at a huge stadium — watching distant, toy-size athletes chase a ball on fake turf, or singers lip-sync into fake mikes — will lose all attraction. And playing sport in a virtual global league, instead of dragging your aging body to a local arena, is inevitable.

This all will occur, not just due to safety concerns, but because the virtual experience at home will be far more vivid and more real than the so-called "real thing."

In turn, as we head into an increasingly home-based leisure society, people will have more time and money to spend on pure family fun.

More Leisure Time

Anything you do online saves you time for something else. Telecommuting or home-based self-employment will free up lots of time and will change attitudes about leisure and entertainment — and about lifestyles in general.

As the rigid, industrial-era, Monday-to-Friday, 9–5 grind breaks down, "work" hours will depend on fluctuating e-workloads and the ability to set your own schedule, leaving more time for leisure. As well, of course, you will save many hours by not going shopping and by avoiding other time-wasters.

The Web Lifestyle obviously is less hectic and less busy, even in a fast-paced, booming economy. Similarly, when the textile industry boomed, the demand for output was persistently huge. Yet most domestic spinners and weavers, being independent and home-based, called the shots. They were relatively free to set their own hours of work. And though public holidays were numerous — making long weekends frequent — many weavers often devoted Sunday, Monday, and sometimes Tuesday to "idleness and sport." While they often worked into the night on other days to catch up, they basically set their own hours, even during the rest of the week. There was no time clock to punch.

A British government Textile Commission report confirmed that "at any moment, they can throw down the shuttle and convert the rest of the day into a holiday." Not that people went very far from home. At most, they would stroll to the village inn or visit a seasonal fair. Otherwise, they made their own fun at home. That was the weaver's lifestyle.

So it will be with the Web Lifestyle in the Internet era. As a

"Webucopia" of games, sports, entertainment, information, and related interactive content funnels into the home, the desire to "go out on the town" will be infrequent. Already, in the wake of 9/11, people are throwing parties at home to avoid public gatherings.

Web as "Social Glue"

At first glance, the Web is de-socializing — we hold images of geek zombies glued to keyboards. Content media such as books, magazines, newspapers, radio, TV, music, movies, and videos are indeed de-socializing. You read, listen, or watch alone, regardless of how many people are around you. The only true socializing while watching TV is to argue over which channel to watch. Otherwise, viewers only "socialize" silently, in their minds, with sit-coms such as *Friends*. Why do you think it's called that?

TV also is a time-wasting device. By contrast, PCs are time-saving "golden looms" that let you get things done and be entertained at the same time. Just as TV took movies out of the movie theaters — their number plunging from 18,500 in 1948 to 8,000 in 1963 — the Web will (as discussed later) literally "de-program" TV. By 2005, more people will interact with PCs than watch TVs and we will — contrary to conventional wisdom — still sit down as a nation for a collective "Web Bowl" experience.

In contrast to the de-socializing, time-wasting TV, the Web — like the telephone on which it is based — is a social medium that extends human reach globally. The Web is the most far-reaching, educationally intelligent, interactive content and entertainment framework ever conceived. As such, it envelops all previously disparate media, converging them into a global multimedium. This multimedium extends all of our senses — our entire consciousness — into cyberspace. Simultaneously, it funnels fun into our Web Lifestyle homes.

Spun to Bits

The Web also literally amplifies all it touches, and nowhere is this clearer than in music. In 1878, Thomas Edison spun a metal cylinder and spoke the words, "Mary had a little lamb," and the contraption recorded and replayed his voice. In 1999, Shawn Fanning wrote the Napster software that allowed free downloads of music over the Web and sent the music industry into a CD-like head spin. It's still spinning!

Fans of every taste have made online music a huge success — much to the initial bewilderment of the recording industry. You now can download or "stream" one hundred songs a month, from a choice of 78,000 tracks, for less than ten bucks.

The music studios have belatedly seen that old media such as 1980s-era CDs — as with cassette tapes and vinyl records before them — are obsolete, spun to bits by the Web. All music studios are feverishly encoding their music libraries for Internet delivery.

Already, 24 percent of North American homes have some sort of "home theater" set-up. Your home theater will organize your downloaded music — as well as video, and family photo collections — into digital albums, distributing them for playing across your in-home network or in the family WebMobile. Flat-panel screen displays of various sizes, scattered throughout the home, will be the Web Lifestyle family's link to the entertainment world.

"VideoWeb" to Kill TV and Videos

The PC is about to swallow the TV. The next PCs will come with built-in TV-tuner cards. Bingo! Bye-bye TV and video stores. Retailers such as Circuit City already are phasing out videos in favor of digital video disks (DVDs), but even those will become obsolete one day.

Today's already-fantastic Web will be a multimedia, interactive "VideoWeb" that could displace most TV content. In contrast to TV, the Web doesn't set the available content. It is a "webertainment" utility where you can get what you want when you want it, not on some preset take-it-or-leave-it schedule. This will become more obvious once interactive broadband is widely available.

Companies such as AOL and Sony are investing heavily in interactive content and will take TV online, much to the ongoing dismay of the networks and cable channels. For example, *Survivor* addicts won't watch it on TV but will chat online with buddies during the webcast program or will call up a synopsis of the last program that they might have missed. And they'll do it while working.

The convergence of movies onto the Web also will dramatically slash the cost of movie production and distribution, delivering the movie to millions of people globally in their homes. Digital downloads will redefine what it means to be entertained and will demand entirely new forms of programming.

As every movie ever made gets digitized and made available for download, video tapes, DVDs, and video rental stores will be "blockbusted" out of business. Your online home theater will know what each member of the family likes to watch and will alert you to new movie releases that will most interest you. No more driving to the video store to search a limited selection and then having to drive the darned tape back again next day.

By 2003, there will be about 10 million people subscribing to video on demand (VOD). VOD will take at least half the market away from video stores within five years. For example, Sony's VOD service, MovieFly, will let you choose from titles that never go out of stock, download them and then view them repeatedly on your PC, or on your home theater via a wireless link. Screenblast, a combo movie-music studio for home users, has editing tools and a library of clips from movies and music soundtracks. You can remix the audio, select soundtrack options, mix-n-match movie scenes, add visual effects, and then play back your own creations.

Interactive Games, Gaming, and Fantasy Sports

The number of people who play online games is expected to reach 160 million by 2004. Family members will play games of various kinds with each other or against opponents around the world. For example, millions of people play just the single game *EverQuest* online.

Sony's PlayStation is geared toward game shows, drawing on its extensive library to provide interactive and multi-player versions of *The Dating Game, Jeopardy!* and *Wheel of Fortune*. This spells the end of TV game shows. Turn those letters, Vanna!

Even gambling is going online. Despite great skepticism — and much spluttering from holier-than-thou politicians who want to prevent it — online gaming is booming. From the Super Bowl, World Cup soccer, and PGA golf, to casino-type games such as slot machines, blackjack, and video poker, gaming is big business on the Web and getting bigger.

So is fantasy sport. Television, having made sports popular, is now killing them. TV has taken sport out of the stadium and trivialized it. Any televised team sport is now like a video game. Everything is contrived and artificial — from the turf on up — and timed to suit the commercials.

Professional teams are slowly being replaced by Web-based fantasy teams. Already, 20 million people globally spend more than $1 billion a year on fantasy leagues. Sport is becoming fantasy entertainment and is close to being scripted. As fantasy replaces reality, Web sports fans ultimately will take back virtual ownership of real-world teams.

Fans are anxious for something new and improved. When the Web swallows the TV, at least 100 million "couch potatoes" will become "mouse potatoes." They'll get a Web-full of offerings: instant chat and one-click video clips, player stats and profiles, articles — and sports paraphernalia for instant sale. Online fans no longer wait for evening TV sportscasts. Instead, they listen to the game while surfing or watch a play-by-play "gamecast" on an in-screen window.

ESPN's MySportsCenter also delivers an online package of the day's sports highlights customized to each user's interests and favorite teams. A "Play at Home" feature lets football fans compete with each other by guessing who will carry the ball, how many yards will be gained, and so on. A daily feature of game action in a videogame-like format ranks in the site's top 25 pages.

In the near future, it will be possible to remotely recreate or simultaneously simulate several sporting events on a home PC. For example, a baseball CD will contain 3D renderings of all the players — in any team uniform — along with their movements in exactly replicated ballparks, complete with sound effects. PC users thus will be able to experience multiple, fully animated "live" games, with the CD-ROM being automatically updated online via Web connection to the real ballparks.

The same could apply to any game, including individual sports such as PGA golf tournaments. Virtual reality installations will let golfers practice their swings and then pit their skills against Tiger Woods — all without leaving the family room.

Tripping Out

Families also will be able to "trip out" in their WebMobiles on a variety of entertainment and greatly enhanced educational excursions.

Satellite-distributed infotainment will be sent to multiple displays where the driver and each passenger can customize their own content. Each will use voice or touch-screen commands to check their multimedia mail, stock prices, sports scores, or watch individual movies or other content. You also will be able to listen to a reading of daily news stories, e-zine articles, or any of thousands of e-books. This content will be downloaded, either overnight to the car in the garage or while driving along.

Already, kids can play video games or watch movies on backseat displays. More than one-third of car buyers say they want an entertainment system in their next vehicle. The main applications will be videos and games played alone or with other passengers. Through Web links, passengers will be able to interact with family or friends back home or with people traveling in other vehicles, sending messages back and forth and playing games together. As well as keeping the kids entertained, of course, software titles and Web-based reference sources can help them with their distance education courses and online degree programs.

For holiday travel, mapping systems are already commonplace. However, a Webmobile will let vacationers enjoy a guided tour through almost any facility, on the spur of the moment. For example, if you spot an exit sign to Gettysburg, you could download a detailed guided tour that plays on cue, based on your car's precise satellite-determined position as you drive along. As you go past Little Round Top you'd get a history lesson and as you drive by Pickett's Charge you'd hear cannon shots, and so on, for a truly real-time, Disneyesque experience.

Doesn't a Web Lifestyle sound like lots of fun?

7
CYBER WORSHIP
Congregate Online!

As with Galileo's telescope, the Web changes the context of life and will again alter belief and how people practice it.

Before organized religion, the home was the center of spirituality. Now, in-home multimedia screens are replacing pulpits and stained-glass in communicating spiritual doctrines and stories.

Going beyond TV church and televangelism, today's Web-savvy click-n-brick church, synagogue, temple, and mosque is already delivering words of wisdom in streaming-video format over the Internet to futuristic families at home

More than a million websites — the Vatican's gets by far the most traffic — are devoted to various faiths. Tens of millions of people worldwide go online daily for spiritual readings and prayers. Many people download content onto laptops and PDAs, or print it out to take with them on business trips and family excursions.

These trends will build a powerful cyber-prayer congregation in and among various religions. Indeed, a growing pluralism will gradually break down sectarian barriers as people create their own interfaith spiritual community online.

And "good" will again triumph over "evil."

Transfigured Spiritual Landscape

In the perceptive words of Dr. Forrest Church, senior minister of All Souls Unitarian-Universalist Church in New York City, "the physical landscape of New York and the spiritual landscape of the nation were transfigured" on September 11, 2001.

That "transfiguration" is altering our society and has spurred a huge spiritual resurgence across North America. While attendance has since fallen off somewhat, church attendance zoomed after 9/11, with many people coming back or attending for the first time.

The search for spiritual community also surged on the Web. Millions are going online. After 9/11, more than 40 percent of Web users, many of them first-time online spiritual seekers, either sent or received e-mail prayer requests.

About 25 percent of Internet users regularly look for religious or spiritual information. Each month, some 30 million American and Canadian adults of every creed — from Adventists to Zoroastrians — turn to the Internet for religious expression. This makes online religious material more in demand than popular services such as online banking, stock-trading, or eBay auctions.

The Internet is being used by congregations of all types to strengthen the faith and spiritual growth of their members, to evangelize and perform missions, both locally and globally. In late 2001, Pope John Paul II himself opted for the Web instead of a trip across several time zones. He promulgated a papal document via the Internet for the first time, sent to the people of Oceania.

Cosmic Cathedral of Communion

Online spirituality also is a two-way affair and the Web provides a unique way for congregations to stay in touch with far-flung members — at college, in the military, or working away from home.

Congregational use of e-mail has become a binding element for many faithful. In 90 percent of "wired" churches, religious leaders use e-mail to communicate with members who also exchange e-mail among themselves for fellowship purposes.

Spiritual websites obviously vary in the breadth of what they offer. Some are merely brochure-like sites: photos, information on the time and place of worship; maps and directions on how to reach the church, synagogue, temple, or mosque. Other sites do online fundraising and recruit new members. Some have religious quizzes, games, and graphics that appeal to children, plus online activities for teenagers. Some ministers and lay members teach college-level theology courses over the Web.

Many websites offer intimate faith services such as prayer requests, daily prayer selections, bible study, an "Ask the Pastor" e-mail service, and a virtual tour of the church. Some websites have a "Virtual Rosary" where you no longer need the beads. A New York rabbi conducts a Passover *seder* online from his basement at home. Some websites host dialogues over diverse issues of faith. Others provide links to counseling and self-help organizations of various kinds. Several sites also webcast their religious services in real time, archive them for later viewing, and provide sermons that can be read online or printed out.

Some local religious groups are becoming more virtual than real. And that points to the future of religion. Studies show one in six teenagers expect to use the Web as a substitute for their current church-based experience. In response, "cool" churches already use the term "cyber-member" as they seek a new young breed of spiritually minded surfers who prefer to congregate online.

Thanks to broadband, global online inter-faith congregation will be an "always-on" phenomenon, turning the Web into a cosmic cathedral of communion and community congregation. In turn, the home will again become the main spiritual hearth, providing comfort and meaning in a vastly changed outside world.

No, the Web won't replace the high-touch, face-to-face, congregational intimacy of traditional places of worship — at least, not yet. But virtual congregations are thriving and their websites provide a sacred space where people can speak freely amongst themselves about religious issues, rather than being "talked at" by their leaders in church.

Personalized Inter-Faith Beliefs

Increasingly, as in other aspects of life, many people simply don't want a middleman between them and their God. And they are personalizing their faith.

Just as the printing press drove the Renaissance and the Reformation, the Web will lead to a transfiguration of world affairs and belief.

With the printed word, the need to hear scripture read or preached about was called into question. Holy book in hand, literate people no longer had to rely on Rome to tell them what the scripture meant. They made up their own minds.

Today, thanks to the Internet, we can almost become a church unto ourselves and customize our belief.

New believers often say they are "not religious" but that they have a spiritual belief and a spiritual need. They want to make up their own minds about what to believe. These growing millions of people feel alienated from established religions, which they see as rigidly dogmatic. They would never set foot in a place of worship other than perhaps to study its works of art.

For them, the Web is becoming their hallowed ground; it offers them the best-connected place where they can explore and satisfy their spiritual needs. Webcast religious services provide such members with front row seats where they can whisper loudly among themselves about what they have just heard.

More than 60 percent of spiritual surfers say the availability of online material encourages religious tolerance and 35 percent believe the Web has a positive effect on the spiritual life of others.

For many people, their beliefs are a blend of several traditions. They explore and learn about various beliefs, latching on to those aspects of each that make most sense in a changing world. Web-savvy spiritual searchers go to inter-faith websites such as BeliefNet to learn and dialog with others as they compare various beliefs.

In an increasingly pluralistic world, people of all faiths are neighbors. Learning about other religions is simply part of being a well-informed citizen. Our own faith can grow wider and deeper by encountering other beliefs and by learning from them. In fact, we can't understand the world without having such knowledge.

And that knowledge is all available on the Web.

The "Infinite" Internet

Millions of people also now talk of their general online experience itself in spiritual terms.

That's the finding of Sherry Turkle in *Life on the Screen*, a study of human identity vis-a-vis the Internet. When interviewed by *Time* magazine for its "Jesus Online" cover story, she also said, "People see the Net as a new metaphor for God."

They see the Internet evolving by "a force" they neither understand nor control, as with life itself. She observes that the Internet is self-organized and, like God, is a distributed, decentralized system.

For sure, how people think of God has changed with the times:

- **Stone Age:** God spoke from Mountaintops
- **Agricultural Age:** God was God of Nature
- **Medieval Age:** God was spoken of as a King
- **Industrial Age:** God seen as Great Designer

Today, God can be seen as an ever-present G-Force — a supreme "WebSource" of networked knowledge, visible in and through the web-like global fabric that connects humanity.

Since the Web mirrors society, it becomes a spiritual manifestation of a new theology. The Web is our theology because the Web is us. It is an extension of our brain-mind consciousness — of our soul — into cyberspace.

So, yes, it is indeed very possible to pray and worship online.

And as we rediscover our spiritual sides online, we will come to better understand ourselves and each other and will rediscover and refine our optimism.

In turn, out of the shadow of the Manhattan canyons of death caused by the gross evil of 9/11 should emerge enormous and lasting goodness.

After all, goodness never changes. And prayer should remind us of that. At least, that will be so, if we pray like we mean it — either at our place of worship, wherever we happen to be, or online at home.

8

VOTE ONLINE
Click the Rascals Out!

Democracy is not dead, but how we conduct it is obsolete. The "dimpled chad" recount fiasco of the 2000 U.S. presidential election is but one small symptom. The 9/11 aftermath and the ongoing War on Terrorism will shake domestic politics at its roots.

All truly democratic nations will eventually move to e-voting from home. In turn, disenchanted voters will be drawn back to participatory democracy, or "partocracy," and turnout will double.

This will go far beyond electronic town halls to ultimately create a real-time process that replaces status-quo parliaments and inconvenient ballots.

The Web will let us revive and embrace Abraham Lincoln's revolutionary, three-part rallying cry for democracy:

> That these dead shall not have died in vain;
> That this nation, under God,
> shall have a new birth of freedom;
> That the government of the people,
> by the people, for the people
> shall not perish from the earth.

Then we'll restore democracy atop a family-based political agenda —

mediated on the Web — that underpins national and homeland security in a globalized world.

Aspiration for Participation

In the unfolding information society, people are less and less satisfied with the existing order of things. Their chief desire is for self-realization and personal growth, and for participation in the management of *their* social, economic, and political system. After all, as Abe Lincoln also said:

> Any people anywhere, being inclined and having the power, have the right to rise up, and shake off the existing government, and form a new one that suits them better. This is a most valuable, a most sacred right — a right, which we hope and believe, is to liberate the world.

In short, we have the power — and the right — to install a new political system more suited to the Internet era.

Back in the agricultural era, people were too busy scratching out a living under feudal lords to worry about any kind of democracy. Indeed, there were no democracies. In medieval Europe, most people knew little about ideas circulating in the world beyond what their village priest selectively told them. Throughout most of the industrial era, the "hard day's work" of meeting everyday needs and then, later on, the pursuit of material consumption, were the focus of attention, again overriding any demand for active political participation.

America and Canada must move to participatory democracy ("partocracy") if politics is to be effective and survive. A demand for political self-fulfillment is coming from a Web-informed electorate. The more informed people are, the more they want to participate in decisions that affect them, not just elect decision-makers. As well, there is a rising demand for political accountability; people want another lever (other than voting) over their political leaders.

This is reflected in political activism. With the rise of special interest groups and federations of different issues movements, once-inclusive organizations — such as political parties and trade unions — no longer provide a sense of identity. New voters want leaders who care more about solving problems than debating party ideology. Party politics is being superseded. And the major political issue today is between the keepers of the old order — who want to keep the *status quo* — and those wanting a new, more participatory society.

Non-Participation

Ironically, as more and more citizens across the globe gain the right to vote, fewer North Americans are exercising it. Only 40 percent of eligible American voters even bother to register to vote, and only half of those actually turn out on Election Day.

Voter turnout in the 1896 presidential election was 79 percent. By 1920, admittedly in the aftermath of World War I, it was only 49 percent — a drop of 30 percentage points in only 24 years! Since then, the peak turnout was 63 percent in the Kennedy election of 1960, but this dropped to only 49 percent in 2000. Turnout also is well below that of most well-established democracies in parliamentary elections.

Voter apathy, cynicism, poor voter registration systems, and the inconvenience of having to "go" to vote are root causes of low voter turnout. People are angry and frustrated with an unhealthy political system that they reject as unfair, untrustworthy, and less relevant to their increasingly self-reliant lives. Two-thirds of voters feel that government is run by a few big interests, that officials don't care what people think, and that they have no say in what should be done.

Even improved registration systems have not helped much. The so-called "motor voter" process, enacted in 1993 and implemented in 1995, did not solve the problem. This made voter registration part of the driver's license renewal process. It registered another 11 million voters in time for the 1996 election, yet the turnout was the lowest since 1924. The process is still inconvenient and anyway is of no help to qualified voters who don't have a driver's license — duh!

Why do we make life so complicated? It is astonishing in this day and age that people are even required to register to vote. Database technology allows us to know who are eligible and where they reside. They should be automatically registered and notified by mail or e-mail when, where, and how to vote — preferably at home. That way, there is no excuse for not voting. Since so many voters choose to stay home on Election Day, why not just let them vote there?

Non-Representation by Special Interests

We also suffer from poor representation, further excluding us from the political system. Voters at large do not choose their representatives; they are chosen for us by their close friends who nominate them. If we could pick the candidate of our hearts, there would be a broader range to select from. Voter choice thus is limited to a very narrow field, championed by special-interest groups (SIGs), political action committees (PACs), and other organized minorities.

For each of the 535 members of the U.S. Congress, there are 40 registered lobbyists and $3 million in annual lobbying spending. A bewildering array of minority-interest SIGs and PACs has more political influence than the majority voters. These groups heavily influence those who bother to vote and tend to support incumbents — regardless of party! Then, once elected, the SIGs push the politicians to pander to their interests.

In 1998, for example, 98.5 percent of U.S. House incumbents were re-elected. They ran unopposed in 95 districts and faced only token opposition in another 127 districts. In the 2000 election, the parties basically abandoned 95 percent of races to incumbents and concentrated all their money and attention on fewer than 30 contests.

Now, it's good to re-elect an effective representative. But most of the so-called majority-decision election outcomes clearly are a farce, if not a *coup d'état*. A democratic façade is created by the few people who bother to show up, the final outcome being determined by special interest voters.

Once elected, in the U.S. or Canada, the so-called "representative" retreats to the feudal-like castle — the Capitol in Washington or Parliament in Ottawa. Ensconced there, they forget the constituents and join an elite oligarchy surrounded by lobbyists that suffocate democracy. "We the people" never rule. Special interests rule.

The SIGs have hijacked the political system and blurred party distinctions. Issue politics has replaced party politics. Hence most voters see no party difference. While this could be unifying and positive, there is a real danger that this effectively could bring a totalitarian-like system that rules by dictate of minority-viewpoint SIGs.

Electoral Reform

To try to purge U.S. politics of special interests, the McCain-

Feingold Bill attempts to overhaul campaign-finance laws. This passed the Senate in 2001 by 59 votes to 41. But the House refused to touch it until 2002, and only then in the aftermath of the Enron debacle and related fund-raising scandal, finally voting 240 to 189 in its favor. In turn, the Senate again passed the modified bill 60 to 40 and the President promptly signed it.

The final Bill limits contributions and personal donations. In the 1999–2000 election cycle, the national parties raised $495 million in so-called "soft" money, the bulk of it from just 800 donors. The bill thus tilts the balance away from incumbents towards new challengers. The larded incumbents didn't want it because it would render them out of office. Even then, it doesn't take effect until at least the 2004 elections and anyway is being challenged in the courts. As well, the bill could be watered down by regulators at the Federal Election Commission.

If fully implemented, such a law would help stop today's "shakedown" operation where party bigwigs and incumbents demand more money from SIGs in return for future considerations. Most politicians are money addicts and the system is so corrupt that it is no better than a mutual protection racket that is destroying democracy. McCain-Feingold is no cure-all, and whether its measures will stop the money-grubbing is doubtful. But it will move politics in a different direction.

In the end, we the people have to take back our political system and reform it. It belongs to us and we need to re-determine how to practice it. A variety of electoral processes need to become more widespread so that we — not the SIGs — can each express our opinions on all the major issues.

To that end, the use of instant, online public opinion polls, referenda, ballots, and so on, will eventually lead to real-time electronic voting from home. As Senator Daschle observed in debating the campaign finance bill, "the currency of politics should be ideas, not dollars." Then, government can again be "by, of, and for the people," as Lincoln prescribed, not "of, by, and for *some* of the people," as Daschle put it.

"Web-Informed" Voters

Much of this trend is driven by Baby Boom and Gen-X knowledge workers — a new political class increasingly demanding a platform of Information Age policies. Most of these people are as smart as their elected representatives, if not smarter. Some 60 percent of the workforce already in North America, this group makes its living from knowledge, usually using computers, especially the Internet.

With millions of home computers at their disposal, citizens can understand both the nature and the implications of the problems arising on almost any issue. Computers provide people with power over their governments — power to police politicians and to tap into the world's many databases that affect government decisions.

Knowledge workers have already exercised immense political power by forcing political parties to address popular issues such as ecology and disarmament, regardless of political stripe. Their dissatisfaction with non-representative democracy will, sooner rather than later, bring what Alvin Toffler in *Third Wave* called "partocracy" fully to the fore. As well, with the move to self-reliant values, and increased emphasis on independence, there is a growing frustration with bureaucratic inaction and complicated legislation.

Instead, there is a movement towards simpler and decentralized self-government.

While centralized bureaucracy is not about to disappear, its limitations are clear and it goes against all the trends. In every progressive society, there is a shift away from large-scale corporate economics to individual entrepreneurialism, from investing in infrastructure to investing in human capital, from confrontation to co-operation, from isolationism to global interdependence. The Internet will change politics in capitalist and socialist societies alike, educating voters about the issues and providing for more intelligent election outcomes and increased voter participation.

Mindless Politics

The old media has helped destroy the system by failing to educate voters about issues. Rather, they merely focus on trivia, scandal, and sensationalism. Even if they acted more responsibly, the increased volume of information prevents them from reporting what's really going on. So they tend to "tabloidize" everything.

This leaves most citizens so dazed and weary that they don't understand the issues. In 1988, for example, one study found that most eligible voters couldn't name more than one in three candidates nor their position on more than three issues. Feeling left out, North Americans generally don't bother to understand the issues or get to know the candidates.

That situation can be changed through better information via the Internet. The more uninformed the electors, the more poorly are they represented. The same study found that less than one percent of voters feel equipped to vote intelligently on the issues. Instead, most vote based on party, name recognition, personal appearance, or the candidate's sex, race, or religion. Voting is haphazard and mindless.

This is no way to govern. Apathy, passivity, spectator-like non-involvement, and mindless voting all invite abuse of power. If we are to have candidate representation, then we must make it possible for all citizens to vote intelligently. Informed constituents will produce more intelligent and more accountable leaders. The University of Utah studied how computers might enhance intelligent voting. A computer voting model, tailored to the average voter, was tested in the 1986 electoral race in Salt Lake City. A panel of experts evaluated the candidates on 60 of the most important issues in the campaign. After the election, the voters filled out a questionnaire to ascertain their own position on each issue. The computer compared their views with those of the candidates to see how they reflected voter concerns.

This analysis was given to each voter and they were asked how this evaluation, had they seen it *before* the election, might have caused them to vote differently. Only 15 percent said they would vote the same way again!

In other words, the voting intelligence of the public can be dramatically raised with an inexpensive piece of computer software. Yet fuddy-duddy politicians and policy geeks complain that if you let people vote on issues over the Web, those voters won't know enough about the issue. In short, pinhead politicians think we the voters are dumb. We need an *Internet Voting for Dummies* book — not for the voters but for these bumbling legislators.

We need to "click" these idiots out of office.

Real-Time Democracy

The Internet is fast creating an environment where citizens can comprehend more deeply both the nature and the implications of any issue. The Web provides independence from traditional media, bringing more information, at a faster pace, to more people, who have a greater ability to understand and analyze it. Government perception of public opinion no longer depends on the upward flow from the grassroots constituent through to the elected politician.

One-way mass media impedes democracy, making us passive spectators in the drama of our own affairs. We don't want to just listen and watch. The new political order is the new communications order — the Web — and today's politics is too cumbersome to keep up. Our so-called leaders are out of sync with the times and with those they are supposed to be leading. The political party that can't interact with the citizenry can't govern.

We are stuck in a time warp where imagery, five-second "sound bites," and "breaking news" transcend the party politics of it all. As McLuhan forecast, whatever is "hot" gets most play. The old media focus on the crisis of the present — never mind "yesterday's news" — and constantly "spin" us dizzy.

As a result, the sound bites are not sound and they lobotomize any reasoned discussion, turning politicians into "invited guest" commodities. Similarly, TV talk shows offer non-debates that are structured so that extreme views clash to maximum effect. The resulting shouting matches do absolutely nothing to educate the public. They stupefy any viewer who tolerates the ranting into taking the sound bites and outrageous spin at face value. There is no intelligent discourse.

Televised "audience participation" programs, such as town hall meetings, are no better. They provide an illusion of participation, deluding us that democracy is being exercised. In reality, there is a small, hand-picked audience posing pre-screened questions. Likewise, candidate debates with questions posed by moderators do little to enlighten. In the first televised presidential debate, between Nixon and Kennedy in 1960, Kennedy set the standard that no debate since has ever met.

Today's candidates practice their answers for hours beforehand on any and every possible question. Then we get partisan pinhead analysts and spin-doctors giving us *their* verdict as to who won. They don't want us to make up our own minds. This is no better than brainwashing that plays into the hands of cyber terrorists. We need to step back smartly and kill it, before it kills our democracy.

The Web Erases "Spin"

Thankfully, the Web is replacing TV and will transform politics. Politics now must learn to multitask along with the rest of us — and act promptly — or get left behind. For starters, the Web erases "spin" — pun intended.

The Web is a spin detector that catches lies better than cobwebs catch flies. Rather than entangling you, it lets you explore, sharpen your thinking about, and interact with unfiltered ideas, avoiding the added spin of biased old media.

The Internet lets our voices be heard, not just during campaign season — which is way too long — but between elections. At precisely the time when today's politicians slow down, we can keep them active. Using the Web, we can keep their feet to the fire longer and then hold them accountable on Election Day. Instead of them giving us spin, we'll make their heads spin and then click them into the recycle bin when they fail us.

On the Web, politics is not local but individualized. It is ours. A fast-evolving e-democracy movement is spreading online and political activism is growing in strength. In turn, a few savvy politicians are taking advantage of the Web's unique benefits.

Nowhere was this better demonstrated than by the election of Reform Party candidate Jesse Ventura as Governor of Minnesota. His campaign used its website to organize rallies, and experts attribute about three percent of the vote — enough to put Ventura over the top — to online activism. This was especially effective in motivating traditionally non-voting young people, plus independents, to come out and vote for him — precisely the people who will reform our political system nationally.

Changing the Voting System

Astronauts out in orbit can vote in Texas elections by e-mail using a secret password. The first astronaut to do so voted in the 1997 election from the old Russian space station Mir. Surely we don't all have to go into orbit, on a foreign spacecraft, before we can vote online? If we can vote from space online, then we should be able to vote on Earth online. Rain or shine, none of us will go out to a polling booth on Election Day 2020 because the system will have been changed.

Changing the voting system is not new. The U.S. voting system has changed constantly over 200 years. Early elections were held by such crude methods as dropping beans into a box. In the 1800s, ballots were pre-marked by political parties, making the voter a mere conduit for straight-ticket party voting. The first election machine came into use in the 1870s. The first ballot to show all candidate names was adopted in 1888. Today's most common voting machine uses long-obsolete punch-cards, commonplace in business in the 1970s. More recently, we've seen postcard mail-in voter registration, mail-in absentee ballots, and vote-by-mail. In some states, as many as nine different election systems are in use.

It's time to get rid of paper ballots of every kind and go digital. E-voting has been tested in the U.S. and abroad, and several countries plan further tests of online voting. They include Belgium, the Netherlands, Japan, Ireland, and Norway. In the U.K., big cities such as Liverpool are adopting e-voting using PINs (personal identification numbers) over a wireless network in municipal elections. And the national government is testing voting via digital TV, telephones, and text messaging. It plans to adopt e-voting nationwide in general elections by 2006.

In North America, public support for e-voting is strongest among those who have the greatest access to and familiarity with the Web. Indeed, students and busy professionals are among the most tech-savvy and yet they are less inclined to bother to vote. Online voting is what they want, and it inevitably would encourage their greater participation.

A poll by ABC News in 1999 found that 61 percent of 18 to 34-year-old voters would vote over a secure Internet system. This compares with 39 percent for the population at large. Such voter popularity will only rise as Web access approaches TV usage. This seems such a "no brainer" that one wonders what dimwit politicians still need to know for them to make this happen.

Secure e-Voting Systems

The usual worrywarts fear the Web isn't secure enough and might be subject to tampering. These usually are the oldest members of society who are always resistant to any kind of change. Not surprisingly, the ABC poll found that 81 percent of those aged 65 and older would oppose e-voting — even if they believed it was secure from fraud!

Of course, only 16 percent of retirees use the Web and most of them don't even know what it is. Many of these are the same biddies who voted twice in the Florida election and were understandably confused by Palm Beach's non-idiot-proof "butterfly ballot." It's no surprise they don't trust voting systems they don't understand.

Yet secure technology exists that would prevent double voting. In the 2000 election, the Department of Defense used a "Voting Over the Internet" program and proved that it is possible to use the Web for safe and secure voting. Virginia lets voters go online to update their registration using a PIN.

Voters thus can easily be qualified, either with secret PINs, as used with banking machines, or with a secret password. After all, if a PIN is good enough to look after your bank account in secret, surely it can let you vote in secret. An e-vote is secure, can be audited, and there can be no false or double voting. And since passwords used by Amazon customers have proven to be fail-safe over a five-year period for processing credit card transactions, isn't that good enough for voting? What are we waiting for?

In fact, both major U.S. political parties used the Web for their own internal voting in 2000. Alaska state Republicans used the Web to conduct a presidential straw poll. Arizona state Democrats used the Web in the state primary and boosted voter turnout by a huge 676 percent over 1996. No, that's no typo — 676 percent!

With the Webolution, the aspiration of a critical mass of voters to decide their own fate is growing in intensity. This G-Force will gradually transform politics into a true partocracy of real-time electronic participation "of, by, and for the people" early in this century.

And partocracy will be part of a Web Lifestyle.

9
BUILD e-WEALTH
Start an e-Business!

One billion prosumer families — "webpreneurs" — will be the future's main wealth creators.

Families used to produce and consume most of their own products; they were "prosumers." The family home was a hive of activity and the mainstay of the economy.

But the economic ties that traditionally bound families and generations together have, with the Industrial Revolution, slowly frayed to the breaking point. And so now the economy is reverting to being home-centered.

In the West and globally, most people do not work for big companies anyway, but for small firms. And most new business start-ups are owner-operated, family-run enterprises, with a surge in such business formations since 9/11.

Knowledge workers are quitting their outmoded and unsafe office-tower cubicles. They are shifting to commute-free self employment and/or home-centered businesses, often over the Web.

Millions of families will become legally incorporated e-business partnerships. Many of these Web enterprises will make their members rich beyond imagination, underpinning the next economic boom and redefining economics itself.

Home-Based Webpreneurs

To achieve truly independent financial freedom for themselves, their children and their grandchildren, futuristic families will use the Web to start an online family business. In turn, these webpreneurs will redefine capitalist ideals.

Economic success comes in a variety of ways. For most people, it has been through blood, sweat, and tears — working for somebody else. Every day, as we saw in the chapter on telecommuting, millions of otherwise intelligent people are forced out of their homes by a comical socio-economic disaster called "commuting" — a disaster most would prefer to avoid. They'd rather lead change than be led around by the nose on a short leash by a boorish boss.

Let's face it, you rarely can become wealthy when working for somebody else. Think about it: most well-off people own a business. They write their own paycheck. So stop building someone else's dream; build your own!

While the skeptics will say, *"I can never do that,"* a growing number of success stories say, *"Yes, absolutely I can do that!"* They have a clear vision of what they aim to do and believe they will attain their dreams. They get on with living the future; they commit to living free. They're a new generation of wealth builders.

The wealth created by the Web will far surpass that of the last several generations of commerce. And it will happen faster than before. Look at how long it took these four people to earn their first billion:

- Henry Ford   Ford Motor   23 years

- Sam Walton   Wal-Mart   20 years
- Bill Gates   Microsoft   12 years
- Jeff Bezos   Amazon.com   3 years

Now, few of us will become billionaires. But the trend clearly is towards many more people generating more wealth faster, especially now with the Webolutionary network effect of e-commerce.

The prosumer boom will lead this trend. And you either want to be part of it or you don't. We could see the first billionaire of the prosumer network economy by 2010.

The Home-Based Tradition

Home-based businesses drove the economy long before the first corporation and the Industrial Revolution came along. As mentioned earlier, the first "manufactures" were handmade by craftsmen at home.

And in the textile era, where families often had a handloom in each cramped bedroom, they upgraded frequently to new and better machines. Sound familiar?

Those entrepreneurs generated huge increases in profits and ploughed them back into the family business to expand output and improve efficiency. They had no shareholders other than themselves and so did not worry about quarterly results or dividend payments. Most surplus cash was reinvested in their business, not spent. They built the business and became affluent.

Indeed, many weavers branched out and became builders of new and improved weaving machines and made house calls to service overstressed machines. These were the world's very first engineers and software programmers. Many of them later were in great demand, as weaving moved out of homes and into factories, becoming plant engineers.

Even before the textile era, almost everyone owned their own family business. They owned farms, ran a blacksmith or shoemaker's shop, or had a small general store in the village. These were all home-based businesses. The farming family lived smack in the middle of their farm. The smithy often lived behind his shop. The shopkeeper lived over the store. And the weavers put their handlooms in their bedrooms.

That compares with today's home-based business: instead of living *over* the shop, you probably live *under* your office — in a spare bedroom or loft studio — and have an easy, 30-second commute, mug of fresh-brewed coffee in hand. What bliss!

Café Latté Networks

While business is coming back home, as in times past, necessary face-to-face business dealings often occur at local coffee shops.

As described in Bryant Lillywhite's *London Coffeehouses*, coffee shops were once an essential hub of commerce. In the 1600s and 1700s in Europe, young men went to coffee houses to get plugged in to what was going on. The coffee house was like today's Internet café or Starbucks. Entrepreneurs and others used the coffee house as their mailing address and as a place to learn the latest news on commercial, political, scientific, and literary happenings. Places of real-time debate, coffee houses became the primary vendors of news; even newspapers were distributed there.

Lloyd's of London actually started as a coffee house frequented by merchants seeking the latest and most accurate shipping news. Yes, the Lloyd's coffee house was "a portal" — pun intended. It became the central place in London for finance and insurance. So it is with the Internet, which plays an altogether similar role.

The network of today's webpreneurs is partially in the real world and partially online. Their real-world infrastructure is composed of copy and printing shops, office business supply stores, mail box centers, courier services, bookstores — and coffee shops. It is a network infrastructure, not a centralized factory full of rows of machinery or an office tower full of rows of desks and cubicles.

Coffee shops, as in Europe long ago, are the place where many client meetings occur. For example, it is estimated that numerous real estate transactions are finally signed off between the parties in coffee shops. This network is overlaid with the Internet as the supreme means of finding information, finding clients, and networking with others. For example, work sent to print shops often is sent over the Web and delivered back to the home office by local courier. While you wait, you can pull up a virtual chair at the IdeaCafé website and get loads of information on starting and managing a business, including e-commerce. Latté, anyone?

What Kind of Business?

There are hundreds of home-based business opportunities. Every 11 seconds, somebody new starts a home-based business — that's 50,000 a week! Of those who already own home businesses, 81 percent say they like the freedom and having control over their own destiny. Making money actually was a motivator for less than 50 percent of them. But a whopping 93 percent say they have no regrets and that they would do it all over again.

You need to find opportunities that suit your goals and which can be highly profitable. You have four main options:

- **Be self-employed** with a stand-alone niche business.

- **Be an affiliate** for an e-business such as Amazon.
- **Be a franchisee** with a franchisor like McDonald's.
- **Be an independent business owner or representative**
  — a form of "private franchising" in a network or
  multi-level marketer (MLM) such as Quixtar.

Let's briefly review each to give you some idea. You need to do much further research on these four options yourself to evaluate which one might be best for you.

• Self-Employment or Stand-Alone Business

To launch your own stand-alone business, you must offer either your own unique skills, perhaps as a consultant, or a unique product or service that meets a unique customer need. You can be very successful by filling an unmet need or niche, marketed over the Internet. But there are few such opportunities and you also need a broad set of business skills to run your own business effectively. If you possess such skills, then you can easily generate a six-figure income for you and your family. People who "go solo" tend to be "income producers" who want to work for themselves rather than work for a salary. They don't want the burden of managing other people or the running of a complex company. However, they tend to hit an income ceiling that they can only rise above by expanding their business. In that case, they become a "business builder" and would perhaps be better to consider MLM.

• Become an Affiliate

You can become an affiliate for online companies such

as Amazon or eBay. In Amazon's case, you can feed customers from your website to theirs, earning a commission on any subsequent sales made by Amazon to those click-through customers. On both Amazon and eBay you can also open your own specialty niche online store or boutique that sells your own line of merchandise. However, the income opportunities as an affiliate are limited and competition in the niche product market is fierce. So the number of people earning sizable incomes on eBay and Amazon is small.

• Become a Franchisee

You could buy and manage a franchise outlet. Franchising is big business and the best franchise opportunities require a lot of upfront capital. The returns can be very high if you acquire a big outlet, and you can become very wealthy. But a McDonald's franchise can cost $1 million for a single store. The market also is becoming saturated in North America and growth is slow except for new franchise concepts. Many such new franchises require a smaller investment, but you will need to work tirelessly for a relatively lower return. Still, if you prefer a defined structure that will help you succeed in a business about which you perhaps know little, then maybe franchising is just for you. Established companies provide a proven model which, if you follow it, should succeed.

- **Network or Multi-Level Marketing (MLM)**

In my view, MLM is by far the best home-based business opportunity for the vast majority of people. It offers a proven model that needs little or no capital, you can decide how much time to invest, and yet you have a duplicable franchise-like business that you can grow. Running an MLM e-business is not onerous. Start-up costs are low, you have no employees to manage or pay, you have no inventory to manage, and no office overhead — in fact the cost of your home office may be a tax deduction. You need to be wary of illegal pyramid operations that falsely claim to be legitimate MLM or network marketing. If the program rewards you for sales made to people you recruit, not just for bringing in recruits, then that plan is legit MLM. You must sort the wheat from the chaff through your own due diligence as to what is legit and as to which MLM offers the best growth and income potential. MLM is for "business builders" who see it as not just a source of income but a vehicle for creating value — that is, wealth. A true business builder will generate more income and wealth than an "income producer". They do this by leveraging the time and energy of others on a team that focuses more on marketing and business building than simply on sales. All you need is a laptop and a dream.

MLM Captures the Prosumer Trend

The global direct sales industry generated revenues of $84 billion in

2000, $28 billion of that in America and Canada. Not all that comes from MLM-type businesses, but some of the world's biggest corporations now use network marketing techniques. Examples are MCI, Sprint, Colgate-Palmolive's Princess House, Citicorp's Primerica, and Gillette's Jafra.

The clear online MLM leader is Quixtar, which got off to a very fast start and is growing rapidly, topping $816 million in sales in 2001, in only its second year. After first-year sales of $518 million — versus only $148 million by Amazon in *its* first year! — Quixtar not only survived the dot-com shakeout but became one of the few big online winners, ranking seventh among all U.S. shopping websites and second in Canada. And it has been profitable from the get go, paying out $143 million in bonuses to independent business owners (IBOs) in 2000 and another $230 million in 2001.

Other large MLMs include Avon, Mary Kay, Herbalife, and Unicity. They were slower than Quixtar to exploit the Web but each of these firms offers huge opportunities to those who commit their futures to them. When you join one of those select networks, you determine your own income based on your efforts, skill, and desire. You become your own boss, work when you want, and with whom you choose. Obviously, the more time you commit and the faster you learn the business, then the faster you will grow your sales and your income will multiply.

Every day, multilevel or network marketers sell — just on the Web — about $200 million worth of vitamins, beauty products, phone services, cleaning products, insurance, and other in-demand consumables. In terms of annual profit, a 1999 survey by *Money* magazine found that most home-based businesses *gross* between $100,000 and $500,000. The average *net* profit of an individually owned MLM business is about $58,000 — double the average workplace salary — and many achieve that by working part-time in their business. A big MLM company generally yields more income, depending on its compensation plan and bonus structure.

The big bonus, of course, is that you get to spend more time at home with your spouse and children and can become more involved in their lives. Indeed, many spouses work together in the business, doubling their chances of success.

As it grows, MLM will become a larger and larger part of the overall economy, particularly as more and more people become prosumers and buy their products and services online — often from their own family-owned MLM e-business.

To grasp the difference between consumers and prosumers, please take a few minutes to study the following self-explanatory comparison matrix.

Producer	Consumer	Prosumer
Own Business	"Rat Race" Job	Own e-Business
Full-Time Boss	"No Time" Worker	Set Own Hours
Operating Profit	Annual Salary	Residual Income
Re-Invest in Plant	Spend Income	Build Wealth
High Overhead	Over Head in Debt	Low Overhead
Expensive Office	Commute to Office	Home Office
Costly Inventory	Empty Pantry	Real-Time Orders
Many Workers	Demanding Boss	No Employees
Pay Dividends	Bonus — Maybe?	Keep it All & Invest
Sell to Consumer	Buy from Producer	Buy from Yourself

Leveraging Network Economics

If you decide to go the MLM prosumer route, you need to leverage the network effect that will grow your business.

Network marketing in particular has the potential to grow exponentially, according to "Metcalfe's Law" of network expansion. A network grows inexorably because, as it expands, its value increases for all its members, thus attracting still more members and growing to the mutual benefit of everybody in the network.

For example, if you are the only person in the world with a fax machine, it has no value to you. You can't send or receive a fax to or from anyone else. Once somebody else gets a fax machine, the two of you can fax back and forth all day. But your two-person network still has little value. As more people get fax machines, however, the network expands and the possibilities of faxing become much larger. Now your machine is becoming really valuable, to you and others in the fax network.

Another simple example is the airline system. If there were only one airport, you could only go on sightseeing flights and then come back again. There's nowhere else to go until other airports open; then the value of the system becomes obvious and the network expands.

That's how Metcalfe's Law applies to MLM. While not a franchisor like McDonald's, an MLM is a network of essentially "privately franchised" individuals. MLM business builders recruit salespeople to further grow their own sales network *and* the larger main network of which they are a part. They "duplicate" themselves through others by sponsoring or franchising them into the MLM. In turn, they earn a commission for franchising them plus a percentage of their subsequent sales. Thus, in MLM, everybody wins as the network grows.

Assuming you are doing MLM over the Internet — which today is the only sensible way to go — what type of person should you try to recruit? Clearly, if you want them to buy from you online, then it helps if they have an Internet access device, are already online, and have bought something online at least once. In short, they know what the Web is all about.

You don't want to be training people how to buy a PC, to use it, to surf, or to shop online. People who can't do that yet are not ready for e-commerce, even though they might be good salespeople. So you need to pre-qualify the prospect on those scores. In short, let AOL and Amazon train your prospects for you — and then recruit them. Don't waste *your* valuable business-building time with those who don't yet, or won't soon, qualify for e-commerce, even though the technology is constantly becoming easier to use.

Define Your Own Future Success

To grow your business, you also need to set goals. But do not overshoot or undershoot in setting targets. If you set unrealistically high goals and fail to meet them, your team will lose heart. Set goals too low and you'll fall behind the market and also lose heart.

If you're running an e-business then you need to leverage Metcalfe's Law of exponential growth. If e-shopping is growing by 50 percent a year, then you need to grow at the same rate in order to harvest your full market potential. In setting your overall target, you also need to set individual targets for each of your prosumer business builders and for each of your passive customers so that, in the aggregate, you will meet your overall growth objective.

Then you need to manage your business against those targets by analyzing sales reports regularly. That will reveal which of your pro-sumer business builders need help. You can also cross-sell and up-sell both the prosumers and the consumers in your business that are falling short. If sales fall behind and you fail to address it, then you will not catch up and will fail to meet your overall target for the year. Conversely, if you can get most of your team members ahead of tar-get on a cumulative monthly basis, then you will exceed your goals and keep everybody motivated.

In short, you must set high standards that define habits of suc-cess. You need to define your future success in your own terms and then look for those same high-level criteria in others that will help you build your network. Do all of these things conscientiously and deliberately and I virtually guarantee you will succeed.

In an overall sense, prosumerism will define what it means to be successful in the new future before us. And when you own and build a Web-based, prosumer-driven e-business you will be successful and wealthy enough to give yourself and your family the ultimate Web Lifestyle.

RE-VISION YOUR FAMILY
Get a Web Life!

On September 11, 2001, we entered a life-altering 20 years of dramatic change. In this new and uncertain world, there are two absolute certainties:

- The **"War on Terrorism"** will continue for 20 years and more; and
- The **"Webolution"** also will continue unabated for at least 20 years.

Indeed, the Web provides the way out of today's uncertain and seemingly contradictory dilemma.

- The Web lets us **"cocoon"** in snug, safe, comfortable environments and yet function very effectively without having to foray into unsafe places.
- The Web lets us **"connect"** with each other, the world, and the future, so we can avoid isolation yet keep our families secure.

While home is a cocoon, the Web-connected home is not a place apart; it takes us out into the world.

Blending these two aspects into a Web Lifestyle, we won't go back to the old "normal" but will create a new and "better normal."

We will "get a web life" that is safely home-centered, yet cyber-spaced and globally mobile.

The Future-Proof Life

Nobody can deny that the terrorism attacks of 9/11 destroyed more than buildings and 3,000 people and their family's lives. They pierced a big hole in America's self-absorption in a globalizing world — a world that was as stunned as we were.

When anything is ruptured, it doesn't just mend but get stronger. The ruptured abdomen, the broken bone, the patched tire, the darned sock, or the stitched garment is stronger where the mending has taken place. Without such repair, the torn whole remains weak.

BandAids cannot repair our punctured, isolationist lives; we must change, by resolving to lead civilization to a true globalization of humanity.

September 11 shattered a sense of security that we took for granted. We now know that we are vulnerable. Neither two wide oceans nor $300 billion a year in military spending can protect North America from vulnerability. No government can guarantee our 100 percent safety.

Being vulnerable nationally and globally, we need a personal zone of safety, a cocoon. And that cocoon is our home. But the key to feeling truly safe rests on a web of human connections. And that means creating a safety net of family, friends, faith, and community. But you can't live a Web Lifestyle by staying inside your cocoon. You also need to get out in the world and connect.

To create our safety net, we need to recover personal control and gain a sense of mastery over our future. We need to "future-proof" our lives. We need to clean out our past, shake off our narcissism, and rebuff the trivial and inane. We need to summon up our resilience and combine it with greater awareness of the G-Forces at play in the world. Then we can have a sense of self within the overall scheme of things and can find positive ways of adapting.

A networked citizen is never alone. Fast-growing Web usage shows just how adaptive we are and how social are our lives. We need connections, and the Web is the mediator between cocooned isolation and global connectedness. We need a Web-mediated life.

As a result of the G-Forces of change discussed in this book, people are taking a hard look at their lives and how they have been living them. Today's modern family and the next generation of families will secure their own freedom and our collective democracy by living the Web Lifestyle.

A Web Lifestyle family will be one that wholeheartedly embraces the Internet and adopts as many as possible of the "Nine Ways of the Web Lifestyle" outlined in this book. Its members will

1. Telecommute.

2. Shop from home.

3. Bank and manage their wealth online.

4. Home school their kids.

5. Doctor themselves at home.

6. Create much of their entertainment in the home.

7. Worship and congregate online.

8. Vote and participate in politics from home.

9. Run a home-based family enterprise, likely online.

Making the Shift

Adopting a Web Lifestyle requires many changes. And change is never easy. But the need to change is indeed as necessary as refilling your gas tank. Even such mundane habits have to be rethought.

Habits that we may want to change can be tough to shake when they are ingrained in the daily routine. So we tend to cling to the familiar until change becomes essential — like now.

As revealed by the Chinese twin characters for "crisis" (*wei-ji*), change is a mix of both *wei* ("danger") and *ji* ("opportunity"). Opportunity comes when crisis stops you in your tracks. It makes you look, listen, think — and start over.

To begin, during time of trauma and high stress, it is especially important to be intentional in how we go about our daily lives and how we think through what needs to change. We've been shaken to the core of our beliefs and must rethink them.

To change your life, then, you need to recognize the need to change and that embarking on a new stage of life is essential to a happy and successful family lifestyle in the fast-changing world. Making changes amid chaos can carry big risks. But clear thinking lets you see what you couldn't see before, lifting your eyes to a new, shining horizon.

Our views sharpened by the knife of the terrorist attacks and the coming "Web War," the "To Do List" of our lives needs to be re-entered on our Palm Pilots with a purposefully pointed stylus.

We need to chart a new "life stream," in league with the G-Forces of the networked society, that combines the things about which we care most deeply. We need to pay attention to life balance — spiritually, emotionally, mentally, and physically — and to stay in touch.

Our future will best be defined by overcoming fear and avoiding isolation — overcoming fear of danger and of change itself, and avoiding isolation from our common community. Fear of change is most often the fear of the transition stage rather than fear of the end result. When John F. Kennedy was assassinated in 1963, many thought the nation would never recover. But it did, of course. It always has. And it will again. This too shall pass.

A "Better" Normal

What emerges will be a changed society. A nation might indeed, as President Bush said after 9/11, define its times. But it can't avoid, as he claimed, being defined by them. We can't, as he urged, go back to normal but can only go forward to a new, "better normal."

What was "normal" on September 10 is beyond retrieval. Yes, we will go about our daily lives. But we will do so in very different ways and with a very different mindset. People are irrevocably changed by catastrophe. Whenever I now walk past or into a skyscraper, I admit it is with some trepidation and in memory of the horror inflicted on innocent souls on September 11.

Every time I hear or see an airplane, it automatically triggers my mind to replay the horror we all watched unfold that morning. Whenever I fly, I now feel much more secure, but I am always on the alert and it will never be the same as before. Nothing can ever be the same again. And if 9/11 was what erupted out of "normal," then I for one don't want that "normal" back again.

What is "normal" always and constantly gets changed anyway to a "better normal." For example, slavery was once considered "normal" in America. It was "normal" that women couldn't vote. Segregated dining rooms, buses, and schools were all "normal." But we embraced a different kind of normal that made America a better place. We've shown that we can achieve a "better normal."

A key step in making a change is intention. If you intend to do something, you set about doing it. Of course, you can procrastinate and try to keep things as they were. But that leaves you trapped in the past, in the "old normal." We must move forward. As the Chinese say, "The long march begins with the first step." So you must intend to change; say you are going to change — and mean it.

That takes passion, courage, and wisdom. Lin Yutang, in *The Importance of Living*, said that "reality plus dreams equals wisdom" and that the three "mature virtues" of a great person are passion, courage, and wisdom. Lin said that without passion we have nothing to start out in life with. Courage, he says, is born of "understanding life" — that is, wisdom. Those who understand life are always brave, while wisdom that does not give us courage is not worth having.

Bigger Dreams

We need to summon our courage to encourage others, intensify our passion to impassion others, and enlighten our wisdom to enlighten others. We need to find a deeper ground for our being that enlightens us to envision the future with new eyes and emboldens us with the passion to achieve new dreams.

We need simpler but bigger dreams and simpler but better lives. True dreams are about future living. We need to envision a different future and our place in it. And the decisions we make will shape the resolve of our character and determine that future.

We need to identify and draw strength from what proved unshakable amid what tumbled down on 9/11. Where is the strength that prevails? It is our rock-fast resolve and our enduring faith in our future — in the American Dream that now becomes the American Cyber-Dream — which we must at all costs prevent from being hijacked into another terrorism nightmare.

This is not a matter of making New Year resolutions and then letting them lapse within a few hours or days. We need permanent and definitive change that takes us to a different place, to a "better normal" for you and your family.

The Trumpet Summons Us Again

As JFK inspired us in his 1961 inaugural "trumpet call" address, we must wake up to the reality that we live in a very small world in which all of us are interrelated. Let the following extracts be our watchwords in this new century.

> The world is very different now. For man holds in his mortal hands the power to abolish all forms of human poverty and all forms of human life.
>
> And yet the same revolutionary beliefs, for which our forebears fought, are still at issue around the globe — the belief that the rights of man come not from the generosity of the state, but from the hand of God.
>
> We dare not forget today that we are the heirs of that first revolution. Let the word go forth, from this time and place, to friend and foe alike, that the torch has been passed to a new genera-tion of Americans — born in this century, tem-pered by war, disciplined by a hard and bitter peace, proud of our ancient heritage — and

unwilling to witness or permit the slow undoing of those human rights, to which this Nation has always been committed, and to which we are committed today at home and around the world.

Let every nation know, whether it wishes us well or ill, that we shall pay any price, bear any burden, meet any hardship, support any friend, oppose any foe, to assure the survival and the success of liberty.

To those old allies whose cultural and spiritual origins we share, we pledge the loyalty of faithful friends. United, there is little we cannot do in a host of cooperative ventures. Divided, there is little we can do — for we dare not meet a powerful challenge at odds and split asunder.

To those new states whom we welcome to the ranks of the free, we pledge our word that one form of colonial control shall not have passed away merely to be replaced by a far more iron tyranny.

We shall not always expect to find them supporting our view. But we shall always hope to find them strongly supporting their own freedom — and to remember that, in the past, those who foolishly sought power by riding the back of the tiger, ended up inside.

In your hands, my fellow citizens, more than mine, will rest the final success or failure of our course. Since this country was founded, each generation of Americans has been summoned to give testimony to its national loyalty.

Now the trumpet summons us again — not as a call to bear arms, though arms we need — not

as a call to battle, though embattled we are —
but a call to bear the burden, of a long twilight
struggle, year in and year out, "rejoicing in hope,
patient in tribulation" — a struggle against the
common enemies of man: tyranny, poverty,
disease, and war itself.

Can we forge against these enemies, a grand
and global alliance, North and South, East and
West, that can assure a more fruitful life for all
mankind? Will you join in that historic effort?

In the long history of the world, only a few
generations have been granted the role of
defending freedom in its hour of maximum danger. I do not shrink from this responsibility — I welcome it.

I do not believe that any of us would
exchange places with any other people or any
other generation. The energy, the faith, the devo-
tion, which we bring to this endeavor, will light our
country, and all who serve it — and the glow from
that fire can truly light the world.

And so, my fellow Americans: ask not what
your country can do for you — ask what you can
do for your country.

My fellow citizens of the world: ask not what
America will do for you, but what together we
can do for the freedom of man.

Finally, whether you are citizens of America, or
citizens of the world, ask of us here the same high
standards, of strength and sacrifice, which we ask
of you.

With a good conscience our only sure reward,

> with history the final judge of our deeds, let us go
> forth, to lead the land we love, asking His blessing
> and His help, but knowing that here on earth,
> God's work must truly be our own.

We are party to a mass transfiguration of world affairs. And we must rise together, family by family, to grasp the promise of our new, trans-figured future as a unified trans-global human family.

The best that history could say about us in 20 years is that we

- won the Web War and defeated global terrorism;
- changed our lifestyle, for our own sake and others; and
- took the necessary steps to a better life in an uncertain world.

It's time to start living the future. And I hope you'll embrace the Web Lifestyle and take some or all of the "Nine Steps to a Better Life" explored in this book.

Every day is a new beginning. Tomorrow is the first day of the rest of your life. Let it be a "Web Life" for you and your family.

Have a super-fantastic, future-proof future!

And thank you for taking time to read this book.

FURTHER READING

This book was researched almost entirely online. A few books are mentioned in the body of the text, but otherwise a detailed bibliography is impossible to provide.

However, this "Top 10" list of books — all classics — particularly enlightened my thinking and I recommend them as further reading. The most instructive are the McLuhan and Toffler masterpieces.

Bell, Daniel. *The Coming of Post-Industrial Society: A Venture in Social Forecasting*. New York: Basic Books, 1973.

Castells, Manuel. *The Rise of the Network Society*. Malden, Mass: Blackwell, 1996.

Gates, Bill. *Business @ the Speed of Thought: Using a Digital Nervous System*. New York: Warner Books, 1999.

Gilder, George. *Life After Television*. New York: W.W. Norton, 1994.

Kuhn, Thomas S. *The Structure of Scientific Revolutions*. Chicago: University of Chicago Press, 1970.

McLuhan, Marshall. *Understanding Media: The Extensions of Man*. New York: Mentor, 1964.

Masuda, Yoneji. *The Information Society as Post-Industrial Society*. Washington: World Future Society, 1981.

Negroponte, Nicholas. *Being Digital*. New York: Random House, 1995.

Tapscott, Don. *Growing Up Digital: The Rise of the Net Generation*. New York: McGraw-Hill, 1998.

Toffler, Alvin. *The Third Wave*. New York: William Morrow, 1980.

INDEX

ABOUT THE AUTHOR

Frank Feather is a renowned global business futurist, best-selling author, and an accomplished public speaker. In 1979 he coined the now well-known phrase "Thinking Globally, Acting Locally" which he converged in 1993 to create the "glocal" concept. He is ranked by *Macmillan's Encyclopedia of the Future* (1996) as one of the "Top 100 Futurists of All Time," a list that includes Leonardo da Vinci.

In 1980, he organized and was Chairman & Director General of the "First Global Conference on the Future," sponsored by the World Future Society of Washington, DC. Still the largest conference of its kind ever held, it drew 6,000 attendees from 56 countries and had more than 1,000 speakers over a five-day program of multifarious topics.

Formerly a strategic planning executive with three of the world's biggest banks — Barclays, TD, and CIBC — in 1981 he founded Toronto-based Glocal Marketing Consultants. In demand worldwide across all industries, he consults to global corporations such as GM, IBM, Nokia, Nortel, and Shell. As well, he has advised the IMF/World Bank, the United Nations, and the governments of the United States, Canada, and Mexico. He has been a Special Advisor to the Chinese government on economic modernization and market reforms since 1984. Even the world's big consulting firms regularly pick his brain.

Mr. Feather's book *G-Forces: The 35 Global Forces Restructuring Our Future* met wide acclaim in the U.S.A., Canada, and Japan. His 1993 book *The Future Consumer* was re-issued in 1997 due to popular demand. His *Future Consumer.Com* was on the bestseller lists at Amazon.com for many weeks in 2000 and has been published in several languages.

Frank was born and raised in Yorkshire, England, immigrating to Canada in 1968. He is married to Tammie Tan, a native of Shanghai, and they have two daughters, Melissa and Ashley. They try to live a "Web Lifestyle" to the extent possible described in this book.

You may contact Frank Feather by e-mail via:

www.Future-Trends.com